Hazard,
Form,
& Value

Hazard, Form, &Value

by Sister Mary Francis Slattery

Mount Saint Vincent-on-Hudson, New York

Wayne State University Press, Detroit, 1971

Published simultaneously in Canada
by the Copp Clark Publishing Company
517 Wellington Street, West
Toronto 2B, Canada.

Library of Congress Catalog Card Number 77-161073
International Standard Book Number 0-8143-1455-4

To My Father

Contents

Preface

 Many years ago while investigating the literary theory of Alexander Pope, I assembled and isolated all of his references to his own excited response to literature and to other things, and I chanced upon a common denominator. In all instances there was a certain feature of the literary object or the situation to which Pope responded that seemed to occasion affectivity. Moreover, the same feature was lacking in literature that he found dull.

At the time I made a brief explicit formulation of the idea which was implicit in Pope's observations. I found that it was a feature of the organization of elements in structure that was seen to be "graceful" and that it had its function in the very definition of the graceful. I subsequently encountered the same feature turning up in different ways in other esthetic qualities such as beauty, the sublime, the tragic, and the comic, in literature and the other arts, and in life situations, evoking excitement in people. Moreover, in the more astute pronouncements of theorists on artistic form I noted that the feature I speak of (which I call the "affective hazard") was always implicit. It seemed to me to be indispensable to the understanding of form and its effect.

At the same time, the discourse of writers on value (in a variety of fields: linguistics, literature, ethics, psychology, physical science, jurisprudence, anthropology) seemed to invite new exploration. They were seeing the indispensability of system. It seemed, in fact, that to understand value at all, one would have to understand system, "structure," or "form."

Accordingly, the lines of reflection in this essay converge upon the dependence of value upon form and the dependence of form upon hazard. The treatment of value, like that of form and hazard, is not exhaustive. Moreover, any observations about literature, painting, music, or architecture are brought in only to provide illuminating examples, and the essay does not claim to be exhaustive in any of the arts. It belongs in the realm of general esthetics, and even there the focus is on the dependences mentioned above, that of form on hazard and of value on form.

I am indebted to Sisters Mary Patricia Dengel, Francis Dolores Covella, Caroline Wall, and Joseph Rosaire McKevitt for their generous encouragement through difficult phases of the work. I am happy too to have an opportunity to thank that rare man and teacher under whom I studied some years ago at the Catholic University of America, Professor James Craig LaDrière, professor of Comparative Literature at Harvard University. Like others among his students, I find my indebtedness to him to be perennial.

Affective Hazard

*W*henever any two things are related in any way whatsoever, five elements are present: (1) the thing that relates; (2) the thing it relates to; (3) whatever is common to them; (4) factors present that are not common and that tend to keep them distinct and separate; and (5) a mind which apprehends the relationship between the two things and, implicitly, their separateness.

The word *thing* can be misleading; it is enlisted for the lack of a word that covers all unifiable terms. Related "things" might be aspects of things, moments of time, ideas, sounds, shades of color, meanings, numbers, practically anything under, or over, the sun. Moreover, in concrete situations of relationship, it is rarely, if ever, found between only two terms. Usually there is almost bewildering multiplicity of relationship.

Sometimes the discovery of a common bond between things is exciting, or "affective," and sometimes it is not. When it is affective, the likelihood is that "hazard" conditions their union. Element (4) is relatively great. The condition that is present when affectivity is experienced can be expressed in the formula: The greater the sum of all that is NOT common to terms that have something in common, and hence the greater the obstacle or hazard to their union, the more exciting or affective the apprehension of their union; or, the more unrelatedness there is, the more exciting the discovered relatedness is.

Thus, when the sum of differences between two things of which a likeness has been glimpsed is great, the affectivity accompanying cognition (of the likeness) is considerable. Alexander Pope implies this idea when noticing "a comparison . . . at once correspondent to and differing from the subject." He remarks:

> To say truth, it is not so much the animal or the thing, as the action or posture of them, that employs our imagination: Two different animals in the same action are more like to each other, than one and the same animal is to himself, in two different actions.[1]

One might compare Achilles' crouching posture at this moment to the crouching posture of a lion before it springs on its prey. Achilles' crouching posture is a result of his accumulating fury; a lion's crouching posture at the moment before springing is the result of its accumulating fury. But accumulating fury "equals" accumulating fury; therefore, Achilles "equals" a lion at this moment.

Here are two different animals in the same action. The aspects of dissimilarity (the sum of terms not in common or the span across dissimilarity, all the nonreferring terms) are great and numerous. The gap between this unique instant in this unique battle of this human hero, and the instant in the struggle of a nonhuman being somewhere in some jungle, is broad. One instinctively recognizes that it can be an obstacle to the finding of a relation between the two terms. One must find each of the two terms, and at the instant before springing, not simply two general terms. This renders their agreement, once found, spectacular. In other words, two terms related by natural affinity, glimpsed for a fleeting moment across distances or obstacles to relation and then gone, are, Pope says, "more like to each other." But are they? Pope means that the likeness is apprehended as sudden and striking. When relation appears fleetingly and unexpectedly, it seems to be very volatile, as though inundating the crevices of the unrelated.

The distance of the span which would naturally separate the two terms which are found related, is, then, very important to affectivity or the impact of feeling produced. The word *hazard* is a better label for the sum of terms not related than the word *span*, because these intervening obstacles are not necessarily spatial or temporal; they simply constitute all the chances against the occurrence of a relation's being glimpsed. Hazards are of different kinds, in our common experience of life "outside" art objects, as well as in the arts. In fact, by the very nature of the case they are necessarily unique and unprecedented. Still, we can conveniently categorize in a large and loose way, if only initially, to make acquaintance with the idea.

The hazard to union constituted by the passing of time is one kind. Henry James, to write a suitable preface to a new edition of *The Aspern Papers*, which had been published many years before, reread the novel and found taking it up again in later life to be very enjoyable. In the preface he described his response as a delight in "the past fragrant of all, or of almost all, the poetry of the thing outlived and lost and gone, and yet in which the precious element of closeness, telling so of connexions but tasting so of differences, remains appreciable." And then he reflected:

> We are divided . . . between liking to feel the past strange and liking to feel it familiar; the difficulty is, for intensity, to catch it at the right moment when the scales of the balance hang with the right evenness . . . the appeal . . . residing doubtless more in the 'special effect,' in some deep associational force, than in a virtue more intrinsic.[2]

This is an apt illustration of my subject. In James's rereading, as his mind registered once again the meanings that were freshly returning, it was as if two widely separated periods of time were brought together, the time then present to him and another time long before whose joy now came back to be felt in a "closeness" that was "precious." The anticipated obstacles to the novel's permanent validity, constituted by his own maturing process, inseparable from the passing of time, did not destroy the effect. The thing was still meaningful, and therefore its interest was excitedly estimated as doubled.

James sensed some richness inviting exploration in his gradually clearing focus upon something explicitly *not* the novel. The appeal resided more in something extrinsic to the novel. In what then? There are only two alternatives: one, that it came from within James himself, and the other, that it was traceable to the continuous extrinsic quantity of time itself.

From his wording, the unidentified ("some") force seems to have been localized by James in his own subconscious mechanism, since he called it a "deep associational" force. Indeed, since the novel was experienced both times in the mind of James, where its meanings registered, there could hardly be a doubt that he did well to designate the mind as the locus of the delight and its force.

However, I suggest that the continuous extrinsic quantity of time itself was indispensable to the force felt in the delight. For now this is the only strand I am lifting from the rich weave of James's paragraph.

Other authors have sensed temporal hazard, too. Lionel Trilling may have been noticing it in his remark, "Whether or not it is made conscious and explicit the historical sense is one of the aesthetic and critical faculties."[3] William Butler Yeats was apparently sensitive to the "vagueness of past times" engrafted upon the real world by "tragic art."[4] Pope, considering Homer, mentions:

> the poet's wonderful art in introducing many pathetic circumstances about the deaths of the heroes, which raise a different movement in the mind from what those images naturally inspire, I mean compassion and pity;

when he causes us to look back upon the lost riches, possessions, and hopes of those who die: when he transports us to their native countries and paternal seats, to see the griefs of their aged fathers.[5]

One of the factors which makes this affective is the temporal hazard. The terms in the case cited from Pope are the boy starting out and the man finishing. The time between these two terms, which keeps them from being identical, is the measure of a life of events that occurred, one after another, and the extensiveness of this series of all the discrete moments of a lifetime charges the moment of death with affectivity. Again, Pope says, "Aristotle . . . calls this a remembrance; that is, when a present object stirs up a past image in the memory, as a picture recalls the figure of an absent friend; thus Ulysses hearing Demodocus sing to the harp his former hardships, breaks into tears." Pope notes elsewhere that in reading a style judiciously antiquated, "one finds a pleasure not unlike that of traveling on an old Roman way."[6] Or again, when "we read Homer, we ought to reflect that we are reading the most ancient author in the heathen world; and those who consider him in this light, will double their pleasure."[7]

Another affective hazard to relation is afforded by vastness of space. If a traveler in Sydney, Australia, getting on a bus one morning, were to meet his own barber from the Bronx, the recognition would be much more startling than it would have been on a Bronx bus, because the chances of their *not* meeting would have been so great in the former case. The mind does not pause to analyze those "chances against" the meeting right at the moment, but they are intuitively apprehended, implied, by the sudden surprise which accompanies recognition. A vast spatial obstacle is overcome by such a meeting, and the hazard is assimilated into their recognition, causing excitement. Longinus noticed Homer's exciting technique in making the vastness of the world the measure of the leap of horses in *Iliad* 5, 110.[8] He tells us, too, "It is grandeur that excites admiration."[9] By grandeur here is meant space, bigness.

Addison, like so many of the critics of his time, was acquainted with the treatise of Longinus and preoccupied with the "great entertainment to the mind" afforded by "vastness and immensity . . . in the wide fields of nature," where "the sight wanders up and down without confinement, and . . . all those scenes . . . are most apt to delight the imagination."[10] It is significant for the point I am making also that Keats intuitively selected a metaphorical reference to the widening out of space before his intoxicated vision in his tribute to Chapman's Homer. Aristotle considered the effect of remoteness to be "fitting" in verse, "for there the subject matter—both things and persons— is more remote from daily life."[11] He says, moreover, that knowledge about the heavenly bodies induces intense joy.

In the case of the spatial hazard as in that of the temporal, the mind simply estimates the extendedness rapidly without really attending to it. And in the estimating or recognizing of the given space, the mind registers the termination of the space. That is, the two terms related to each other are simultaneously glimpsed, although maybe not dwelt upon, by the mind. The vastness of the spatial span between the terms is something fixed in the very nature of reality, and the emotional excitement is assured to the moment of recognition of terms, to the moment of the concept of space, when all its extendedness is stored up in the mind. And such a spatial situation, even only imagined, can be exciting: "Sometimes . . . it is by means of the phantasms or concepts in the soul that one calculates as if seeing."[12]

Numerical quantity acts as an affective hazard, too. When a boy comes home from school with the news that he is first in his class, this news is impressive if there are forty boys in the class; it is less affective in its import if there are only three. The father's mind instantly measures the thirty-nine chances against coming out first, hazards constituted by number. Or when a man is singled out of a whole nation to perform an act for the nation, he becomes news. Our imagination intuits without analyzing the millions who were excluded in the choice of this man. Longinus had said in regard to style that "in certain cases the use of the plural falls on the ear with . . . imposing effect and impresses us by the very sense of multitude."[13] William Butler Yeats refers to poetry and imagination as "always the children of far-off multitudinous things" in an essay which bears the significant title "The Emotion of Multitude."[14] Again, the unifying by the same act of a whole multitude brings irrational tears to the eyes, if a whole stadium sings the national anthem or if a vast cathedral of worshipers sings the *Te Deum*. Numerical hazard is involved, moreover, in the attraction we feel toward watching lines of cadets in lock step. It is the source of exhilaration in the epical plural of the collective national voice at the opening of *Beowulf*: "Lo, we the Spear-Danes . . ." Indeed, it is the complete absence of the rational from the emotional excitement due to numerical hazard overcome that is the butt of Fielding's good-humored mockery in these words of *Tom Jones*, 6, 1: "When I have seen a man strutting in a procession, after others whose business was only to walk before him, I have conceived a higher notion of his dignity than I have felt on seeing him in a common situation."

There is an affective hazard also in the difference of degree of excellence, or authority, or social status, between two people or terms brought into relation with each other. If a peasant meets a king, such a meeting is more absorbing than a meeting of two peasants, because a hierarchical span of separation is bridged. Almost all of us in childhood engaged in the delightful pastime of hero worship, in which, even when the reality threatened to be a denial, we pulled wool over our eyes by stretching the difference between the excellence of our idol and the ordinariness of the rest of men and then contemplated him in his superior eminence. Pope observes in a note to the *Odyssey* how the Phaeacians "could not but highly admire a person . . . who had been permitted by the Gods to see the regions of the

dead."[15] Here the extendedness of the difference between
the importance of the experience of Ulysses and the usual
mundane experience of the Phaeacians caused admiration.
Ulysses himself, he notes, was aroused by the Sirens who
had called him by his name, eager "to be acquainted with
persons of such extensive knowledge."[16] The interest enjoyed in the widening of the distinction between one status
and another is a commonplace. The irrational indulgence
of this in snobbery makes it specious.

Frequently, hazards to the likeness of things referred
to are occasioned by the radical difference in the natures
of the terms related, and these hazards, in metaphor, for
instance, are delicately charged with delight. Moreover,
hazards of different kinds can attend the same occurrence
at the same time. To provide an example of the operation
of the principle of affective hazard in this category, I suggest the obstacles to wit. Wit has long been a disputed
term. I am here using it to mean not invention, nor genius,
nor a metaphysical poet's faculty of gathering together
distant ideas, nor a punster's lure of words for their own
sake, but to mean, as Pope says, "a justness of thought and
facility of expression."[17]

If, in a swiftly passing moment, a miracle of repartee is
achieved by a stroke of someone's wit, the witty sentence
becomes meaningful forever. The nature of the mind, orig-
inator of the witticism, is such that it usually thinks of
the clever thing the next day; or the nature of events is
usually such that they do not, in their complexity, shape
up to give the man of wit his opportunity. Consequently,
when the usual recalcitrancies of the mind and of events
retire at the crucial moment, the witnesses to the clever
retort automatically intuit without analyzing that the
chances against this occurrence of the witty remark were
enormous, and this is what makes the occurrence forcible
and memorable. Even when a witty remark occurs to a
person in solitude, he looks back upon the experience with
pleasure and wishes he could share it, because it seems to
have significance. In this latter case, it is clearly not the

temporal hazard, the fact that it occurs at its only moment in history, a moment on which—let us say—the destiny of a nation depends, that before an audience might have given the fitness an affective charge; nor is it numerical hazard—the vastness of the audience responding to it, for instance, the waiting nations watching the speaker in the General Assembly on television. It is simply the hazard to conception and compression as such.

Natural resistance is felt to be great when what is expressed is very much and words very few, or when the thing meant is evanescent and words somehow fixed. When, in spite of the hazard to efficient management of meaning, a few small words evoke it all, both the words and what they signify seem bettered. A hazard resides in the ratio between the slightness of the sound signifying and the relative magnitude of the signified; or the fixedness of the one and the shifting and vanishing of the other. What is meant by the words seems a better thing than it did before, and the words seem to be better words than they were before. The affective response becomes a sort of applause, and, as Pope says, "nature" is "to advantage dressed." Nature, the thing meant, although often thought before, has been "ne'er so well expressed." John Dewey noticed that resistance to expression offered by a medium of an art can cause a certain emotion in the artist, which has its function in the artistic process.[18] Words being a poet's means, the resistance they offer by their limitations at the moment that this resistance is annihilated in an apt expression excites the poet.

Certain logical distinctions must be observed for the security of the principle of affective hazard. One is that the span between terms, not apprehension of the relation, determines our excitement. Even Aristotle, who was repeatedly very close to perceiving, did not quite see that. That he was close appears in his observation that it is natural for all men to delight in imitation,[19] a statement about the receiver, as we gather from the context of his remark, for he is talking about looking at a picture. De-

light arises, then, from seeing relation between terms
which are not identical by nature. However, I think the
Greek philosopher localizes the cause of affectivity in the
seeing of relation rather than in the intuited hazard to relation seen, because he gives as the reason for the delight
"that one is at the same time learning—gathering the
meaning of things."[20]

Yet it is precisely by close reading of Aristotle that I
claim an ancient corroboration of the principle, because
he lingers on the fact that when the object is not pleasing,
the imitation is. If cognition alone were the cause of delight, then an object so ugly in real life would not be
pleasurable in a painting, either. For in the phenomenon
known as esthetic distance, which is clearly present here,
the interest felt is traceable partly (though not entirely)
to the differentness of the natures of the imitating object
and the thing it imitates.[21] Significantly, too, Aristotle be-
lieved that men from the beginning wondered about things
that were mysterious and difficult to solve and that they
sought to learn them not for any utilitarian value, but
just because they were mysterious. And another pronouncement that the "facts" of a "mathematical argument . . .
are indifferent to us, not objects of either desire or aver-
sion" is, I think, proof that he did not mean that cognition
as such is always affective.[22] Let us imagine, however, a
mathematician at work, seeing a mathematical solution
that nobody ever saw before, the key to a puzzle that has
long baffled his predecessors. The excitement of that moment of his cognition is enormous. What here gives the
conditions of affectivity is the hazard to the cognition of
the solution. Still, in terms of the five elements of a
relationship situation listed at the beginning of this essay,
Aristotle tends to localize the affective stimulus in element
(5), the apprehending mind, and element (3), the grounds
of relatability, whereas I am localizing it at element (4),
the degree of hazard to the apprehension of relatedness.[23]

But another precaution is necessary. It must be remembered that (4) alone, the hazard itself, will not occasion

our excitement. There must be a hazard, but the ignition occurs only at the instant of cognition. Documentation for this also can be found in Aristotle, who dwells on the pleasurable motions of the soul, not only in perception of things present, but in memory of things past and in anticipation of things to come. Even "toils" are "sweet . . . remembered when survived," he quotes Euripides as saying in *Andromeda*; and Aristotle ponders the lines of the *Odyssey* which refer to the delight in rehearsing former grievous woes.[24] These observations secure the realization that the registering of cognition in the mind of the receiver is an important part of the affective occurrence.

That cognition of relation as such is not the affective nucleus, but the "widely divergent" span to be bridged between terms related, is emphasized by the fact that anything, no matter how interesting in itself, grows less exciting as it becomes well known. As Pope remarked in a letter to Caryll, May 1, 1714, "The same thing . . . makes me leave poetry: long habit and weariness of the same track."[25] Habit, by itself, corrodes the span between terms and destroys affectivity that accompanies apprehension of meaning (surely not cognitive meaning, which increases with habit). And Homer was the "track" of which Pope was wearying, Homer who for Pope represented poetry at it peak. Austin Warren, in his essay "Evaluation," says of the esthetic experience that "practicality is one enemy; the chief other is habit, operative along lines once laid down by practicality."[26] He is perhaps too cautious, for habit simply, not the habit of a thing once found practical, is enemy to the esthetic experience. Homer's poetry is not of its nature "laid down by practicality," no matter how many uses civilizations may have put it to. And in terms of our affective hazard, the esthetic experience has an enemy in the frequency which induces familiarity, for familiarity reduces hazards to cognition.[27]

It is noteworthy that one or both of the terms related to each other might be real, or they might be only imaginary; and the glimpse of cognition might be very slight, possibly an undefined intuition. Interrelationships may be those of realities, and the "truth," therefore, or they may not be. Saint Augustine suffered keenly from the fact that the affectivity in the experience of apprehending the meaning of things not true could so bewitch him.

It is not an exaggeration to say that a simple list of all the implications of the principle of affective hazard would crowd a good many pages. Since relation can already be found as soon as there are at least two things in the world and a mind to register them, the most complicated relationship is found to be everywhere by this advanced stage of the world's history. To ask, therefore, just where this law applies is like asking where Newton's laws apply; in fact, application can be made to logical and imaginary matters, as well as to physical existence; and to potencies, as well as to actualities.

Form

It is common experience that after reading the final paragraph of a novel and closing the book in a profound reverie, we tend to remain for some time in the world created by the novelist, exploring and measuring meanings and situations, while the real world around us seems shrunken and unappealing. When we come out of the theater after a performance of *Hamlet*, the city street rebuffs us by its blunt lack of what might be called the far-reaching. Concentration for a few minutes in a quieted classroom, in the initial wrestle with the syntax of a Shakespearean sonnet, and the gradual transition to a state of celebration of infinitesimal perfection leave one in a joyous realm that widens and is felt as splendor. However, something valid gradually fades, then, in the disturbance and the shuffle of moving to the next class.

The contrast experienced is that between unusual awareness and the shallow, fragmentary attention that is given to the tentative and the unrelated. The response to the quality of an artistic form differs from response to the character of the passing through the day's events as form differs from formlessness. The experiencing of a work of art is richer than that of mundane reality. The form of an art object is not continuous with life, although it can successfully create the illusion of being so. It is fundamentally

separate from life and has its own laws, although its elements may include references to realities with their own
particular attachments from life. The art object exists objectively as something made by the artist, having its own
beginning, middle, and end. Its form is imposed upon the
elements by the artist, not the receiver, although the receiver's mind in response contributes something. The
degree of perfection of form seems to determine the meaning and feeling it causes in the receiver, but feeling is not
the criterion of its excellence.

DEFINITION OF FORM

Form, as defined by Craig LaDrière, is "the character
of an object as experienced, or the structure into which
the elements of an experience or a thing are organized."[28]
In including the words *as experienced* and *of experience*,
LaDrière's definition provides for the distinction between
what is in the mind, on the one hand, and what can be in
the world outside the mind, on the other. The form might
be the character of something that exists outside the
mind, a thing, or it might be the structure of elements of
an experience. Nevertheless, regardless of whether a structure is objective or subjective, structure itself, simply as
such, LaDrière defines elsewhere as "simply the totality of
all the relations that obtain among the elements of which
it is composed."[29] Again, "All structure is based upon, indeed is constituted by, relations."[30] To begin there, with
the propositions that (1) form is a totality; (2) that form
is a totality of relations; and (3) that these are relations of
"elements" is convenient, because however flexible, it is
free of the complexity of much modern discussion and
claims no more than what should be assumed in all of it.[31]

Totality, moreover, is an effectual word for two reasons.
First, it expresses the fact that the form is the whole thing,
a form made of forms. The forms which make up the

whole will be more or less numerous and various according to the complexity of the object or experience which presents many or few, different or similar, elements in relation.[32]

A second advantage of the term *totality* is that by maintaining generality and abstractness it is able to allow for what is also true, that the substructures and elements represent bewildering variety, each "making its claim for a specific orientation of interest; . . . each capable of focusing the attention of a different kind of analysis."[33]

The classification of forms as substantial and accidental by philosophers before Hume can be dispensed with in the consideration of artistic form, for art forms as such are only accidental, not substantial. Saint Thomas Aquinas explains the distinction between them:

> The difference between accidental form and substantial form is that whereas the former does not make a thing simply be, but only makes it be in this or that mode—e.g. as something quantified, or white—the substantial form gives it simple being. Hence the accidental form presupposes an already existing subject; but the substantial form presupposes only potentiality to existence, i.e. bare matter.[34]

St. Thomas explains that art objects are accidental forms, not substantial. He notes, commenting on Aristotle's *De Anima* 412a13, that the Greek philosopher makes a distinction

> between physical or natural bodies and artificial bodies. Man and wood and stone are natural bodies, but a house or a saw is artificial. And of these the natural bodies seem to be the more properly called substances, since artificial bodies are made out of them. Art works upon materials furnished by nature, giving these, moreover, a merely accidental form, such as a new shape and so forth; so that it is only in virtue of their matter, not their form, that artificial bodies are substances at all; they are substances because natural bodies are such.[35]

Art thus imposes accidental form on substantial materials supplied, ultimately at least, by nature. Nature's "substantial material" is sometimes directly supplied, for example, the marble of a statue; but frequently the materials themselves—paint and canvas, catgut, steel and concrete—are processed by man; and although sound as such and human organs of speech that produce it are natural and physical, the material of poetry (language) is already intricately conventional and formal. Hence, the tracing of the materials to nature in such a case terminates in something more properly called "ultimate."

The common denotation of *form* is simply the determinate aspects that we apprehend in things. There is "form in things . . . in life and living," Eva Schaper writes.[36] When we notice relationships among events of life and perceive a group of such related things, adverting to their mutuality and thus temporarily isolating the group for our particular notice, we are, as she observes, "formulating." No matter how small a particular mark, gesture, or word may be, if it is seen as related to a system of interrelatedness, it has significance. In life, when we see the connections among things, we apprehend their "significance." Although relatable things, and the bases of relatability, exist outside the mind, the mind does the relating. Nature infinitely supplies the things, endlessly supplies the bases of relatability and infinite varieties of hazard to relationship. The mind, by its own nature, tends to find the relationship and is excited perpetually by the hazardous condition of it. When one notices that a bluejay in flight to the neighboring tree is reflected in the pond, and holds the twin blueness for an instant in the mind, one's curiosity is roused and reaches to find gradations of blue in the sky and then suddenly the mind notices blue also in a flower. This becomes a pursuit, and everything not relevant (not blue) retires from notice: one's own jacket, the length of the shadow of the stick on the ground. This relationship of blue and blue is sought in the almost-blue darkness of shadows among the trees and across the pond, and when it is found concentrated, the eyes are held by it. The exclusion of all irrelevance sets formal boundaries, and the interrelationships among which the notice oscillates is a kind of form. This is Eva Schaper's "formulating." Often nature presents things as complete formulations, and natural forms engage us deeply by their beauty and grace.[37]

MATTER AND FORM

The nature of form becomes clearer when form is considered in its relation to matter. Form is, at any rate, not matter, and consideration of the relation of matter to form has been, according to René Wellek, the great issue in literary criticism. He quotes T. S. Eliot as saying in "his usual noncommittal manner": "It is always true to say that form and content are the same thing, and always true to say that they are different things."[38] For Eliot, the issue was the relation between them in poetry, not the relation of matter and form as such in anything at all. But his unwise use of the word *content* distorted the concept of the relation between matter and form simply as such. The matter is what a thing is made of, and the form is what makes it what it is; "where there is form there will be matter, informed; where there is matter there will be form, informing . . . it is only by their union that the thing exists."[39]

Since the poem is made of words, which are in turn composed of sounds and meanings, sounds and meanings are the matter of a poem. The form is the totality of structures shaped of these—structures of sound and structures of meaning.[40] Thus, the matter has both sound and meaning, and the form has, too, their difference being that matter as such is formless, whereas form is order.

The matter is not always so tangible as pigment and marble, and in the case of a poem where language is the material, "the form . . . includes the forms of language and is . . . conditioned by and dependent upon them."[41] The matter the poets work with has already been given form in four different ways: by arrangement of consonant and vowel sounds; by construction of those into sounds of syllables and words; by attachment of a signification to organized sound to form a word; and by arrangement of these words into syntactical grammatical constructions.

The arranging of consonant and vowel sounds is done by differentiating, just as making the marble into the form of a man is done by separating or chiseling away what in the block of marble is not of man's form from that which is. In the sound there are only differences, without positive terms. In the forming of an unexpressed idea, too, the same is true. The mind focuses on it, "discriminating" or separating from it all that is not it.[42] And the idea in itself is a form.

However, the sign, which comprises the sound signifying something and that which it signifies, is a positive term (sound plus signified equals sign, or word). And a linguistic sign (word) is in itself an infinitesimal form, in which elements are related. Moreover, syntactical and grammatical arrangement is already advanced organization. Even in such grammatical speech whose value is "the simplest communicative efficacy," the form is determined not only by conventional rules of grammar, but by the nature of "the social situation in which it occurs" and the characters included by it.[43] To trace the boundaries and subtleties of such a form even at its simplest is a vast "assignment."

But poetry uses language not primarily for a communicative purpose nor for persuasion but for something else, namely, the making of a beautiful structure as such. The nonpoetic, normal use of speech is implied by the poetic, deviational use, and the poetic has an additional complexity (and a hazard) in that fact. Moreover, although the poet makes the poem of the material that includes forms of language, "literary form is not merely linguistic form,"[44] whose principle is efficacy of communication, but form of which the principle is esthetic.

The beauty of sound structure, although notable in

itself, serves the whole pattern of configuration. Osborne says it emerges as "an intensification of meanings or of the relation among" meanings.[45] This may be traceable to the fact that the mind is at a state of increased awareness in the noticing of pattern and thus discovers meaning, which accordingly gains in intensity. The effect upon the receiver of intense meaning in an esthetically valuable structure is a further increase of awareness. Thus, the beauty of meaning structure heightens that of sound. They are not separate, but mutually constitutive and aspects of a totality. Additional solidarity is perceived as force of felt aptness, that is, relationship that has sustained hazards. Thus, the words, phrases, or sentences in a poem are not the same as the same words, phrases, or sentences in isolation. The whole leaven of words changes. The properties or attributes of sounds and of silence are organized into a structure which makes its own claim upon the mind of the receiver. Even a single sound occurring as an element of such structure is in itself something different from that same sound if it were not a part of the structure. In structure each value keeps its own entity, and yet each becomes a quality of the others.

Stated another way, the form of sound esthetically organized allures and holds the auditory attention, drawing it to unusual alertness. The structural clusters of sound occur, and an individually noticed sound is loved and is surrounded by the glances of the mind. The incantation leads the mind to an attitude of expectancy and satisfaction, a mode different from that of response to disorder. It qualifies the apprehension of meaning by disengaging the mind from normal grammatical structure, which is secure and naturally irregular in rhythm; norms of grammar are implied by the deviation from them, and the deviation, being radical and yet kept near by the materials it shares in common with grammatical structure, is pleasurable. The truant mood of the receiver's mind is observable in its tendency to float freely among contexts. Instead of the confining of the mind to a denotative logical sequence, there is an attending to connotation and suggestion; the notice oscillates emotively among phonetic samenesses— assonance, rhyme, alliteration, prosodic recurrences. Poetic language, moreover, has the maximum of connotation and a minimum of denotation, being at the pole opposite to the logical prose language, whose words have a maximum of denotation and a minimum of connotation. The relatedness among connotative elements of meaning is relatedness among aspects, accidents.

In the unfolding of prosodic structure, relationships are hypothetical, then evident, and gradually become determinate.[46] And poetry is made of language whose expression is linear. Therefore, signified meanings are composed always of consecutive unities. A term thus acquires its significance because it is opposed to that which precedes or that which follows, or to both.[47] In Meyer's terminology, the term's significance, once it is evident, is significant partly because of the hypothetical significance it promised to have before it was expressed; or, if what is expressed deviates from the expected, the new, now evident significance is significant because in relation to all that preceded it, it is presently found determinate. Thus, even prescinding from the sounds that express or signify something in language, the psychic registerings themselves are hypothetical, evident, or determinate. There are three stages: before the expression, the expression, after the expression. When it is remembered that relationship is not made actual at all unless a mind discovers it or makes it, we can reflect exclusively for a moment on the three phases of the mind's operation in the very apprehension of relationship.[48]

In the linear prosodic and syntagmatic arrangements, and in the semiotic occurrences of isolated elements, the hypothetical, the evident, and the determinate are distinguishable, however suffused and rapid. In fact, extending the notice to the field of associative relationship within the realm of linguistic meaning, we can see that hypothetical, evident, and determinate phases occur there, too.[49]

A poetic structure is organized esthetically into its

unique self. LaDrière explains that, although made of phonemes, lexemes, and syntagmatic structures of the language like the product of any literary art, poetic structure differs from grammatical speech, whose virtue is correctness and whose value is communicative efficacy; and its differs from rhetorical speech, whose virtue is eloquence and whose value is its persuasive as well as communicative effectiveness. The virtue of poetic structure is unity, and its value is esthetic. Any structure whose principle of organization is esthetic is a "structure in terms of relation simply as such." It provides the only norms that are relevant "for the apprehension of its form and for judgment of its value."[50]

Paradoxically, the syntagmatic and associative meanings of the language of the poem seem to allure attention when they are elements of structure whose primary principle is not linguistic but esthetic. To the degree that the primacy of the esthetic is maintained, the linguistic meanings become alluring and engaging. Actually, this means that awareness has been increased in the receiver; and although language normally exists as an instrument of meaning, the less the language yields to the ever more exacting demand of the esthetic principle, the less meaning is realized.

As soon as any one orderly occurrence of elements attracts notice, becomes threatened, and wins its hazards, the mind begins to pursue it. Such occurrences may be rhyme, alliteration, assonance, pattern among groupings, cadences, measures, syntagmas, roots of words, prefixes, suffixes, significations, recurrences of words, phrases, refrains, and whole areas of meaning. Form imposed upon such elements gives recurrence and hazard opportunity, since it consists of organization of these, recurrence broadly considered being "sameness" and hazard "difference." As soon as sameness is managed in spite of the infinite variety of hazard, the mind is excited, and hope begins for another occurrence of the same, felt as a potency. And "while a thing is moving from potency to actuality, and as long as it is still in potency, it has a natural relation and inclination towards actuality, and when it attains incomplete actuality it still desires a more complete actuality."[51] Accordingly, the mind pursues with curiosity, the actualization by the form, of further expression of the norm, which, occurring in the thick of potent though gossamer hazards, invites a "fine frenzy" of pursuit. The hazards are the lures of the other actualizations of norms. For instance, where the connotative association of a signification is hypothetical and, as such, still only a potency, the hypothetical hoped-for rhyme might be presenting its own urgency. But this, too, is held in abeyance by the delay of a line's termination, demanded by the stanzaic structure. The rhyme becomes evident in a way that suggests that it almost did not occur. The signification still waits but now with a new hypothetical condition of a possible enlargement. Presently, the long line is terminated, the stanzaic form is evident, rhyme and stanza are seen as determinate, and the unactualized signification is still desired; but the new rhyme of the oncoming stanza holds out an invitation of more complete actuality and hazardously threatens the signification. When the mind quietly discovers that the signification, in disguise, is in the midst, evident, a synthesis of rhyme, stanzaic evidence, and meaning is determined; totality is "felt."

The mind is detached from all else that is not the form by the "emphasis of the rhythm which has been set up within" it, as Roger Fry says,[52] and keeps advancing to attain more complete actuality of the hovering and newly awakening potencies. When an elemental or microstructural occurrence moves from the hypothetical to the evident despite hazards, the mind holds it excitedly and values it. The poem being a system of potencies, it is felt to be a field of hazards, or a condition in which occurrence is found miraculous; each type of order is a hazard to every other, in its apparently casual lure of the notice. The reader's mind is given up completely to being a noticer. Whichever type of order is most subtle, most threatened by aggressiveness of the others, is, provided it is genuine, the one that wins the mind's attention, and all the hazards it has sustained confirm its victory. The celebration is not denied it, even if its claim is only that it is a rhyme, or only a signification, or an evident resolution, or whatever it is. It is not what it is that merits applause, but the miraculous propriety of its occurrence. And the form is the determinant of that. All that threatened it turns to confirmation. Hence, each element gains its unique glory from the hazardous condition of its fitness that form provides, and the form has its actuality in the flesh of the elements. Since the matter is language, the unique glory given it by the form will be experienced as linguistic intensity, as scope of meaning and sweetness of charm of sound, and the form will be a beautiful celebration of these.

FORMALITY

The nature of form appears not only when it is seen in its relation to matter, but when it is viewed in itself, in its formality. Such a view might focus first upon predispositions to formality in the elements, then on unity, and finally upon hazards to unity.

Relatability. Elements are predisposed to formality if they and relatable. If only one thing existed, there would not be such a thing as relation. It is difficult to sustain the imagination of only one thing existing; and once there is more than one thing in existence, things are relatable, even though not related. By using the word *they* for these things, one relates them. If no one ever came to exist and to find them, they would nevertheless be relatable; one, let us say, as an atom of hydrogen and the other a speck of carbon twenty billion miles away. The fact that, unlike the nonexistent, both existed would separate both from nonexistence and find them sharing existence. One would refer to the other on the basis of not-nonexistence. But in getting beyond that bleak phase, to a universe where there are millions of suns, stars, and an earth turning on its axis and teeming with infra-human life, we see that one amoeba is related to another, and in a way in which he is not related to the ocean. One dinosaur is related to another dinosaur, an acorn to an oak, an oak to a cypress, and an oak and a cypress to rain.

Relationship is based on quantity or else on action and passion.[53] A star can be related to another star quantitatively: one is bigger than another, one is a certain distance from another. Again, a developed organism is more an organism than the undeveloped. "They cannot be said to be equal, if one participates in the form more perfectly than another."[54] The dinosaur is related to the water by action, for he desires water and drinks it, and the water submits passively to being drunk. The oak grows, which is its action, and brings forth the acorn, which passively receives its existence from the oak. These relations are real. Real relations might be necessary and inevitable, like that between the father bear and the cub. But again, real relationship between things might be contingent, as when two yellow leaves fall from two separate trees at the same moment when no breeze is stirring. ·

When a human being observes the real relationship between two things, the relationship is not changed but simply discovered. The snowfall coming after the fall of leaves.is related to the snowfall that came after the fall of leaves a good time ago; and after the completion of this snow and thaw, and new leaves and the fall of those, another snowfall occurring is related still more securely to the preceding. It is observed that winter "always" follows fall and is always followed by the spring. The mind discovering this makes a unity of the relationship, isolating it from all its accompanying irrelevancies; sequence is related to sequence. "The essence of relation is being referred to another," Saint Thomas says,[55] and it is the mind that does the referring; it refers to each other two things that reality supplies, on the basis of some relatableness that reality supplies. The laws of physical nature are so guided by necessity that relationships among elements and events are inevitable; they are registered in minds as secure expectation even before they are realized in nature.

The case is different with contingent relationship.[56] The simultaneous falling of the two yellow leaves at opposite ends of the orchard on a breathlessly still afternoon is a relationship between real things, and the basis of their relatability (yellowness, leafness, their falling, and at the same moment) is real. Nevertheless, the relationship is not anticipated, nor is the incident likely to be repeated. It is single and is experienced as coincidence. Although it is real, it is hazardous, the chances against the simultaneous falling being almost prohibitive. Therefore, the noticing of it involves some affectivity, however slight.

The human being's continuous dwelling in the midst of related persons, things, and events in nature and in the course of his life acquaints him with relationship. We understand what is meant by tomorrow or next year, although they have not yet been experienced. The understanding is based upon yesterday and last year and today and this year, which are experienced. When terms of relationship are not supplied, the mind, habituated to discovering them, supplies them. It is the exercise of the mind, among other things, which forms the basis of implication, by which we presume terms not actualized by expression.

Meanwhile, the mind can also supply terms, imagine them, conjure them up before itself, independently of reality. Therefore, when the idea "this winter" occurs, the mind can explore relationship per se, exploring "other "winters" and "next winter" or "winters a million years from now." Or it can change not the relationship but the terms, by opposing them, as when it thinks "summer" or, by supplying alternative terms, "autumn" and "spring." By exercising itself, the mind logically surveys positive-negative, opposite-same, general-particular, complete-incomplete. Relationships are thus made which are not based (directly) upon reality, and thus they are "logical." One can say, for instance, "The leaves fell to the sky." It means either that there were puddles beneath the trees, and the sky was reflected in these, and the reflection of the sky is called *the sky;* or it could mean that the speaker is under the influence of some unusual inner stress that distorts either his mental vision or his speech; or it could be that children are saying it for the fun of absurdity. Whichever it means, it gets the additional implication from the difference between real relationship and exclusively logical relationship.

The basic distinction between real and logical relation is explained by Saint Thomas, who differentiates that which exists "in the nature of things as in those things which by their very nature are ordered to each other, and have a mutual inclination," in one sense; and, in another, that which is "found only in the apprehension of reason comparing one thing to another."[57] The example he gives for real relation is that between a heavy body and the earth. Elsewhere, he notes: "The very order of things created by God shows the unity of the world. For this world is called one by unity of the order, whereby some things are ordered to others."[58]

The neglect of the reality of relation is not healthy for criticism. Hugh Kenner takes note of that fact in a protest against the loss of "intelligibility of things in relation . . . so that there are no *real* relations to be perceived." If the reality of relation is not relied upon, he says, the poet's making of metaphors "becomes merely a sweaty arena for patching and botching."[59] This is not to say that the terms of every metaphor are to be borrowed from reality directly; but should the relationship of the metaphor not be one of reality, and often it is not, the reality of relation is relied upon nevertheless, the existence of the world of reality being the climate in which all literature and all art can have its own effect. Moreover, it might include a healthy share of objective reality.

The subjective is real, insofar as it exists, but by fixing the focus of attention exclusively upon it and thus blinding oneself to objective reality, one loses the ability of seeing the subjective, too. Heller astutely observes in his remarks on Thomas Mann's *Doctor Faustus* that what brings the threat of cultural sterility and despair that disposes a man for a pact with the devil is the incongruity between that which is and that "which can be said."[60] By that "which is" is meant that which is in the depths of the protagonist's self (according to the context). Those depths would of course be chaos if objective reality did not exist; but in that case the chaos would not lead to despair and cultural sterility. It seems to me that it is because one knows that there *is* objective reality that the meagerness of what "can be said" is painful. Moreover, by shifting the focus from the interior of the self to include objective reality, one can even hope for restoration of order in the self. The disrepute in which so many hold philosophy and metaphysics tends to obscure the importance of objective reality and therefore of real relation, in spite of the discoveries of physical science. Be all that as it may, real relation exists, and consideration of it is good.

Although relationship can be found among things in objective reality, and the relatableness seen is founded upon their relatableness in reality, a mind actualizes the relationship and sees the likeness or bond. In that sense, relationship is necessarily in the mind, between mental images of the relatable things. This is true even when we are in so concrete and present a situation as, for instance, that of silently watching a robin carry a worm to the nest. For the robin is not inside our heads; the image is, and at best it is only a partial one. Moreover, if words are used for telling about robins when we are removed from such situations, the whole process is even more clearly removed from objective reality. The meaning of each word is simply an aspect of a verbal sign, a mental image or concept which registers in the mind when the image of the sound (or print) of the word is conveyed to it. Relationship in the mind between the image of the sound and the concept is rendered practically automatic by our knowledge of a convention of language. And when words are strung together in a discourse or in a poem, meaning begins to be actualized in many orbits, so to speak, in addition to that indispensable one between the acoustical image and the concept. It is unpredictable and ephemeral, and in a poem especially it sometimes occurs in many ways at once and is unseizable.

Even were meaning to occur always singly, one might feel defeated by the task of dealing with it, since its scope is virtually infinite. Nevertheless, it is possible to survey alternatives. Abrams, in *The Mirror and the Lamp*, begins by noting simply the obvious fact that all outside the poem is divisible into the universe, the poet, and the reader. Since, moreover, relationship is actualized in a mind, the formidable field so blithely called "the universe" is not unclassifiable. The mind, anyhow, can discover or devise relationships among things in the universe outside the poem, among elements in the poem, between aspects of the poet and the universe, between him and his poem, between aspects of the poet and his readers, among aspects or phases within the reader in his response to the universe, in his response to the poem, between the poem and poetry, between the poem and the universe. Moreover, relationship can be found endlessly in the universe. However, in the practice of criticism it presents little difficulty, since this is not what the poet or critic is obliged to account for, even though its existence is indispensable to poetry.[61]

In spite of the immensity and complexity of the universe, it is possible to divide it into classifications and hence to relate some of its aspects to others. By means of relation, abstraction, and conceptualization, the mind, and consequently language that signifies its concepts, can be used with extraordinary elasticity. For instance, from the heap of terms—of, five, estimating, years, the, the, the, and, and, sun, radioactivity, of, of, chemistry, calculate, of, age, at, men, the, earth, million, changes, by, consequently, be, center, thousand—one can shape the sentence: By estimating changes of chemistry and radioactivity at the center of the sun, men calculate the age of the sun and consequently of the earth to be 5,000 million years.

It is an absorbing sentence, expressing quantitative vastness, implying amazing achievement on the part of men. If it is not true, we are nevertheless quite absorbed by it. When we find it is true (it is thought to be), it puts us into a state of silent exploration. We may think that what we are exploring is truth and that the faculty we are using is reason, but such is not the case; the sentence gave us the fact, and we are exploring the meaning, relating many things to it. The imagination, in particular, is stimulated under the influence of affective impulse occasioned by the hazards of time, space, degree of achievement, and deviation from the mundane, occasioned by the fact.

This is not so difficult as it is entertaining. When two things are related, the affinity is not between one whole thing and another whole thing, but between an aspect of one and an aspect of the other. No analysis of the whole of each is required or even desirable. A blue-green tint in the sky might be seen repeated in the blue-green reflection in the river and the blue-green car on the road. The viewer does not revert to the conditions in the atmosphere and position of the sun necessary for the tint, or the length, width, depth, density, direction, speed, and chemical composition of the river, and the metal, body, engine, and paint of the car. Saint Thomas says that "relations do not import composition in that of which they are predicated."[62] The composition of the whole car, of the whole river, of the atmosphere are not important to relationship. The aspect of blue-green is.

Because this is true, it is true also that the size or complexity of related things in themselves is not the criterion of their importance, but only their relatableness. The simple gesture of turning down a thumb, used by the Roman emperor, could change destinies. Pope in his note to *Iliad* 6, 595 ff. says, "There is a vast difference betwixt a *small* Circumstance and a *trivial* one, and the smallest become important if they are well chosen, and not confused." By *small* here is meant limited in dimension, and by *trivial*, limited in significance, irrelevant, superfluous.

Relevance is the desideratum of a "circumstance" to be included, therefore, and from this, one can see the importance of context. Context supplies more terms and therefore interrelatedness to be joined by a newly added relevant term. Meyer, in his account of meaning in music, says meaning "arises when an individual becomes aware, either affectively or intellectually, of the implications of a stimulus in a particular context."[63] And the more particular the context, the more lure the meaning has for the mind. The reason is that intensified particularity has numerical and qualitative and hierarchical hazards.[64]

Relationship is internal or external. Internal relationship is affinity of aspects of two or more parts of one whole; external, that of aspects of parts of more than one whole. The relationship of father, mother, and children of one family is internal; the relationship of the youngest boy, who plays football, to the boy across town who plays football is external to the family.

When the relation is that between aspects which are "accidents" (as distinct from substance), like the playing of football, or like the blue-green tint of sky, river, and car, then the things of which they are aspects (boy, sky-river-car) are understood, presupposed to be distinct. Saint Thomas writes, "Relation presupposes the distinction of the subjects, when it [relation] is an accident."[65] The very distinction is a hazard; so, if we take imitation as some sort of correspondence, "it is natural for all men to delight" in it, as Aristotle says.

As soon as accidental aspects of two different things are related, they are seen as a unity, and when many aspects of many things are related, they are experienced as still more unified. The "unity and simplicity . . . exclude

. . . plurality of absolute things, but not plurality of relations," Saint Thomas observes. The absolute things are
the substances or entities of things whose aspects (blue-
greenness, shininess) are related. It would destroy the
unity and simplicity of an impression to dwell on carness,
riverness, atmosphereness, but it unifies and simplifies the
impression to explore and oscillate among the blue-greennesses. And the more complexity among blue-greennesses
(complexity arising from the differences of the absolute
things, the numerousness of things reflecting blue-green,
the variety of hue and intensity and light and dark and
values of blue-green), the more the interrelatedness of the
blue-green isolates blue-green structuredness as a separate
whole, a new structure distinct from everything else. It is
a form. It has a nature or whatness of its own. In fact, the
more accustomed the mind grows to seeing this interrelation of blue-greenness of aspect, the more it tends to
reach for more blue-green, and when it keeps discovering
it in its perpetual hazardous vanishing in the blend with
other color, or in shadow, unity is intensified, and the
form becomes the more durable. In painting that has
esthetic value, form is a structure of just such structures,
each making its appeal to the notice.[67]

This is true not only of painting or of all structure
that is static, but even of dynamic structure which is actualized in temporal sequence. The reason is that although
objectively the occurrence of the antecedent is quite finished before the beginning of the occurrence of the consequent. it is not so in the subjective response. The mind
retains the image and impression of the antecedent while
it is receiving the consequent (remembers, let us say, the
promise made in chapter one of the novel), and this is
one of the reasons that the impressions can be apprehended as parts of a form. The antecedent is an actual,
cognitively apprenhendable term. In the receiver's cognitive response, correlatives are simultaneous. Moreover,
what Meyer says of meaning in music throws light also on

the condition of apprehension of dynamic structure in poetry:

> Evident and hypothetical meanings do not . . . arise and function in isolation from one another. Evident meaning is modified by the hypothetical meanings previously attributed to the antecedent. That is, the consequent is not only that which actually follows, but it is that which follows as expected, arrives only after a deviation, resolves an ambiguity, or is unexpected.[68]

So also in a plot the incident which resolves the suspense is not alone what "strikes" the reader: all that might have happened, and all that kept him waiting, is included in the impact of the resolution. The consequent is related (actually follows, arrives) to the antecedent as conclusion of hazard, and "meaning" is absorbing and exciting.

The surrealist, who considers the work of art something whose meaning will not be intelligible until a later time, makes of the object an element only; it is an element whose correlatives in the dynamism of time's ripening are not simultaneous. Hence, it is no actualized relationship, and there is no significance. At its best, its meaning is hypothetical; it never becomes evident and certainly never determinate. This is because relationship is absolutely external rather than internal, the fundamental error of neoplatonist esthetics.

In a genuine poem, rhythmic structures, structures of qualitative sound, of meaning, of micro-structure in the exigencies of the poem, all beckon to the notice of the reader. The macro-structure is necessarily unclear in the sense of being only partially actualized. The unity is simultaneity of relatableness among complexities that cannot be quite exhausted.

Assimilability. In addition to being relatable, the elements included in a form are naturally assimilable. This is suggested by the doctrine of Coleridge as he refers to an in-

nateness of form that is "organic." He says that unlike
"mechanic" form, such as that predetermined pattern impressed on matter from without, "organic form . . . is in-
nate; it shapes as it develops itself from within."[69] But
since, as we have seen, relationships in a structure are not
realized except by a mind, Coleridge's words, referring to
"development" by the form, must be applied to a receiver's mind gradually apprehending form or to the poet's
mind engaged in the process of making it; Coleridge
thought of the poet's mind, his "imagination," as "organic."

The distinction he was really making was that between
the poetic process in which invention and arrangement are
complete before expression and poetic process in which
invention, composition, and expression are exercised simultaneously. Actually, a product of each of these processes can be good. The flaw in form which Coleridge called
"mechanic" is not to be traced necessarily to the arrangement's having preceded expression, but rather to its not
achieving unity. If unity is achieved by either method,
the form is organic; if unity is not achieved, no matter
what the method, the form fails.

In the more likely and probably more universally exercised method, which Coleridge inaccurately ascribes to
"organic imagination," the achievement of unity is notable. What happens in such a case is that when the product
is begun and structure begins to appear, the fixedness of
something expressed has a stabilizing effect, enabling the
poet's mind to get control. His imagination plays synop-
tically among possibilities, that is, elements which are
naturally assimilable and at the same time hazardous and
fleeting. Sometime, in the airy press of these, there occurs
a relationship which is deeply enticing, enough to allure
him to abandon the original plan for something else, and
all the elements of the partially finished structure keep
adjusting in new ways to such enticements. So it is that
the form seems to "develop from within." Actually, the
form is not organic, and the poet's imagination is not;

something indeed seems organic in the sense that something changes from one phase to another in the progress of the poem toward completion. Change from phase to phase is "growth" of organisms. But the principle of such change in the case of a poem is localized not in any organic life in the form, nor in the mind, but in the encounter of the poet's mind with linguistic elements partially structured and their potentialities. This need not be disheartening and dull, once it is realized that meaning is "generated"—simply, it occurs—by juxtaposition of word with word; such meaning can "grow" to such extreme intensity as to induce rapture.

Even in the tight unity of onomatopoeia, which Coleridge so admired, the fact is that the mental image of sound is assimilated to the mental apprehension of meaning. The wonder, therefore, is not the twinning of sound and meaning, but the facile efficiency of the instrument of the mind, performing its characteristic and routine but enormously complex operations.

Art implies choices and very exacting work on the part of the artist. The product is not inevitably brought to completion by any inner necessity of the organism. But the potentialities of the elements and the swift automatic (not necessarily determined) operation of the mind result in a process so ready and facile as to appear inevitable and to make the art object appear to develop by laws of necessity toward ends inherent in the "organism."

Opposition. While elements are predisposed to formality when they are relatable and assimilable, they are so particularly if at the same time they show oppositeness. Frequently, hazards are constituted by opposition of elements in artistic form. Critics repeatedly notice the tension of opposition stressed by Coleridge. We are told that the "best unwritten book on Yeats as a constructor of lyrics will organize his great opposing symbols . . . and will show how they are marshaled . . . for the engagement of each particular poem."[70] T. S. Eliot explains that the disgusting in Dante is "completed and explained" only by the exquisite last canto of the *Paradiso*, Dante having succeeded in "expressing the complete scale from negative to positive."[71] *The Ambassadors* "gathers an intensity" from "the play" of "oppositions."[72] The "more opposed the discordant units of meaning synthesized, the more valuable the resulting fusion."[73]

Every work of art differs from every other, and within each structure the posture of elements changes perpetually. Regarding the nature of opposition, however, whenever it is perceived, there are terms opposed and there is a condition of their occurrence. And the opposition can originate in the elements or in the condition or manner of occurrence.

If the opposition originates in the nature of the opposed elements or the terms themselves, it is because the elements differ in their respective origins, materials, individual manners and postures, and dynamic tendencies. Respectively, for example, the front vowel and the back vowel of neighboring syllables have different origins, the sound and the signified in a word have different materials, the rigidity of the hat and the softness of the hair in the portrait are separate in manner, and their severe horizontalness and downward swirl, in posture; the trochee and iambus have opposite dynamisms.

If the opposition of elements is in the condition or manner of their occurrence, tension is more hazardous. This opposition is a tendency toward terminal separation, dynamically or statically supported, initial or gradual, clashing or centrifugal. The terminal separation is a pull for the receiver's attention exerted by the nature or situation of one element (or perhaps substructure of a total structure) against a pull by the nature or situation of another.

Tension dynamically supported appears in the phenomenon of suspense, for example, and static tension appears in the lyric. Frequently, the two orders, dynamic and static, are played against each other. In James's use of

the central intelligence, for instance, the unifying lens is
turned on dynamic reference, so that a broad static system
(the central intelligence) and dynamic progression of the
events of the novel are in tension. James describes the
result aptly: "Strether's sense of . . . things . . . should
avail me for showing them. . . . It would give me a large
unity, and that in turn would crown me with the grace
. . . of intensity."[74]

Gerard Manley Hopkins noted types of tension occasioned by initial and by gradual opposition. He considered the structures of poetry necessarily to be a continuous paralleling of two kinds, one where the opposition
is clearly marked and the other where parallelism is transi-
tional or chromatic. The clear initial opposition is seen,
for example, in rhythm, the recurrence of a certain sequence of rhythm, in alliteration, in assonance, and in
rhyme, as well as in the parallelisms in thought begotten
by the force of these; also, in metaphor, simile, parable,
antithesis, and contrast. The chromatic parallelism, however, is in gradation, intensity, climax, tone, expression
(as the word is used in music), chiaroscuro, and perhaps
emphasis.[75] In Hopkins' classification of opposed and
chromatic parallels, one is reminded of Roman Jakobson's
dichotomy of "figures of similarity" and "figures of con-
tiguity."[76]

Jakobson's observation that verse gravitates toward
metaphor and prose toward metonymy may, I suspect, be
explained in terms of the contrast between initial and
gradual opposition. In the reading of verse, the dynamism
is oscillatory, and notice is directed to mutual phonetic
reinforcement and to stasis congenial to metaphor, that is,
mutual referential reinforcement. However, the dynamism
of prose is toward progression, and because metonymy
makes less oscillatory demand, being less arbitrary, the
meaning can hurry on. This means simply that the slightness of tension caused by substitution of name (metonymy) is such that it does not quite defeat the tension between the later phases and the earlier in a syntagmatic

progression. Thus, whereas in metaphor (the substitution of both a *signifié* (*res*) and *signifiant* (*verbum*) for another) attention inclines toward the substituted *res* and to substitution itself, in metonymy (the substitution of only the *signifiant*) attention casts no more than a backward look at the substitution.

A characteristic of artistic form is the presence of tension everywhere in it, and tension appears in a great variety of ways. We are told to observe it in "poetic statement, poised precariously between various semantic planes," as Erlich states.[77] In music, uncertainty and delay of a tone is tension, effectual in producing affectivity. In Pound's Canto LXXX, Kenner notes the "studied *incongruity* of image and language whose tensions both climax and resolve the preceding passage."[78] Pound's images are of ruinous greed, but his language approaches elegance.

In general, the tension of initial separateness is provided by time delays in rhythm and recurrence of rhythmic sequence, by difference of sounds in words that are alliterated, by difference among syllables that have assonance, of lines that rhyme, of signification in simile and metaphor, of referential sequence in parable, of connotative direction in antithesis, of effect in contrast; in other words, by difference, simply. Tension in chromatic parallelism occurs in difference of degree, namely, degree of progress (gradation), of emphasis (intensity), of importance (climax), of communication (tone), of externalization of feeling (expression as in music), of clarity (chiaroscuro), of effect (emphasis).

Clashing tension is observable everywhere in musical displacement of one dynamism by another, in meaning structure where human wills are in conflict, in dense saturations and color contrasts in painting. Centrifugal tendencies, however, are in rarefied reference, the pull of connotative against denotative structure, extremities of deviation and of perspective.

The resolving of tension in form results from a newly discovered relation of elements or aspects, or from some redundancy that invites settlement into repose through the attention's relinquishing of potencies, hazards of any kind. At that moment habitual responses suffice, and the receiver rests while still attending. Such a rest is provided by redundancy; or by the unity in subordination of reference or expression. In the structure it appears as unification, resulting in the receiver's renewal of control, the preparation for keener hazard.

Reciprocity. Again, each of the parts of an organic form is, to use Coleridge's expression, "reciprocally means and end," and the "dependence of the parts on the whole" is no more notable than the "dependence of the whole on its parts."[79] The reason this is possible is that the structure is made of relationship actualized by the receiver's mind. To consider the parts as a means to the whole focuses attention on the value of the whole, contemplating it with conscious retentiveness concerning the parts; to see the whole as a means to the part directs the mind to noticing the particularity and extent of the part and at the same time to holding on to the totality that is momentarily in abeyance. The full response to the work of art includes free play between both these modes of attention, teased, so to speak, by the lures of values.

It is clear, then, that relatable, assimilable, opposed, and yet seemingly reciprocal elements conduce to organization. Elements can, nevertheless, be arbitrarily thrown together in chaos. In some buildings, poor acoustics sometimes cause dead spots where no sound is heard; or echoes which clutter musical sound are heard when the pianist keeps his foot on the pedal; sometimes music is transmitted poorly; and sometimes it is drowned out by foreign sound from, say, street riveters and construction machines.

Meyer mentions two kinds of noise, acoustical and cultural. Acoustical noise is the kind just described, in which sound is chaotic and without pattern or integration. The sounds of passing cars, honking horns, chatter, and construction drills are not music. Cultural noise, conversely, occurs if listeners have certain habit responses, and the responses appropriate to the style of the music being played are disparate from these. The listeners experience the disparity as something like noise. Their habit of response does not equip them to respond properly to that music.

In modern music a certain amount of noise results because the composer delays the occurrence of the expected term while rousing other expectations which in turn are left unfulfilled. Thus, one potential meaning obscures another. This obscuring is effected by a constant distracting of the attention from fulfillment of expectation, and expectation remains unfulfilled. The impression is one of frustration, then estrangement and bewilderment, and finally just endurance. Interest awakens incidentally and occasionally, as some fleeting recognition of a pattern seems promised. The totality is tolerated as a symbol of jadedness and sophistication and is redeemed and applauded at unexpected moments of resolution or fulfillment. Modern music is saved and followed for the sake of those moments.

Meyer considers acoustical and cultural noise to be causes of undesirable uncertainty. He defines desirable uncertainty as "that which arises within and as a result of the structured probabilities of a style system in which a finite number of antecedents and consequents become mutually relevant through the habits, beliefs, and attitudes of a group of listeners."[80] The style system becomes a source of probabilities; the probabilities are structurally determined. They bring about desirable uncertainty by creating expectancies which are either temporarily supplanted or noticeably kept waiting.

Hazard is indispensable to interest, but there should be a limit to hazard. This fact must be recognized, because frustration must be limited. The antecedents and consequents must become mutually relevant if uncertainty is to be desirable. Desirability is experienced at the moment of eventual relevance. Experience of desirability

is localized in many persons, namely the listeners, and it
is minds that find relationship. Moreover, the habit of
response, or the belief, or the attitude of the listener disposes him to find relevance. There are degrees of natural
and cultural endowment in listeners. Listeners habituated
to responding to modern music have developed retentiveness to sustain the low redundancy of terms, and such
listeners have attitudes of tolerance, having experienced
some degree of reward. It requires a certain amount of
musical sophistication to achieve the necessary retentiveness. In primitive music, however, a note which was a
deviation from the tonal system turned up only at the end
of the phrase, once the norm had been well established.[81]

The principle discoverable in all experience of music,
as of the other arts, remains the same, however. It is the
principle, already frequently mentioned, that the composition must venture as much complexity as the form is
capable of bearing. It must be almost too much to control. The ratio suggested by the word *almost* is as delicate
as possible. The hazards to interrelationship must be almost insurmountable, and yet they are there for the sake
of terms which they apparently militate against. The
frustration of relationship occurs only for the sake of the
exciting moment of frustration's defeat. The moment of
annihilation of chaos is not thundered or clearly outlined
in the expression, but the excitement, subtle and interior
as it is, is a proof of the form. The interiorness of the
proof derives from the fact that the finding of the relationships is done in the mind; but the mutually related terms
have their basis in the art object which is outside the
mind. The subtlety is based not on the fact that its discovery is achieved by the mind, but on the object's
hazardous organization: it is left at the stage of multiple
potency, unfaded and partially unactualized, but implicitly
determined. This is confirmed in retrospect as order turns
up, miraculously, everywhere in a prolonged dawn. In the
temporal arts of music and poetry, such a gradual discovery of the formal organization of the work is a sort of

"periplum." Ezra Pound gives the meaning of the word in canto 59 of the *Pisan Cantos*: "periplum, not as land looks on a map but as sea bord seen by men sailing." It is, as Hugh Kenner explains, an "image of successive discoveries breaking upon the consciousness."[82]

UNITY

Although many of the statements made thus far have been about form, the main intent has been to indicate the predisposition of elements to formality. Form itself is achieved in the organization of the elements into a unity. Accordingly, each element performing its own particular operation contributes to the singleness (not simplicity) of the whole.

One universal characteristic of organization as such is subordination. In

> all things which form a composite whole and which are made up of parts, whether continuous or discrete, a distinction between the ruling and the subject element comes to light. Such a duality exists in living creatures, but not in them only; it originates in the constitution of the universe; even in things which have no life there is a ruling principle, as in a musical mode.[83]

There is no novelty in the doctrine of subordination nor in its application to painting, poetry, the novel, and architecture.[84] And yet, although there must be subordination, it must not approach obliteration. In the novel, for example, "the image and the sense" of the subordinate part must be kept. It is "a case of delicacy . . . at every turn" to keep art "exquisite" by sometimes summarizing and foreshortening, giving "all the sense . . . without all the substance or all the surface."[85] The dominance of the ruling part cannot be enjoyed if there are no subject parts; and its domination is best when it is seen to have survived the threat occasioned by the noticeable value of a part.

Principality and degree of subordination appear not only among elements, but also in the norms of structure. Lesser norms serve the principal one. Thus, the notion of the *dominanta*, that is, the "dominant or organizing property" was one of the two basic tenets of Russian Formalist theory. The principal norm aids the subordinate: when the border of lace shows by a subtle but actual feature that it has lineage from the central dominance of pattern, it is valued. And, in turn, it specifies the dominance of the pattern; the subordinate aids the principal norm, also.

The dominant character of any process whatsoever, or the way it is done, is dictated by the reason why it is done; its sanctions are immanent. The girl rushes across the gymnasium and through the door if the whole side of the room is on fire. Or she walks slowly, turning this way and that, making a full turn, retracing a few steps, and then walking out, if she is modeling clothing. If she is dancing, she does not make for the door but stays and celebrates patterns of graceful movement.

In the first case, speed is the dominant norm, dictated by the urgency to survive. Subordinate norms would be the fitness of using her feet to run and of watching where she is going. They are followed without being adverted to; but if the way out is obstructed, and she has to crawl on all fours or beat her way through things without seeing (casting aside those other norms because they do not aid the principal), she does not hesitate in her haste. The principal norm dictates the way. If she were to use her feet and watch where she was going (satisfactory for other needs), but abandon the norm of speed, it would be disastrous.

In the second case, the principal norm is that of slow, wheeling progression, dictated by the purpose of showing the dress for a few brief moments from every angle. If the subordinate norm of being pleasant (which answers another requirement) were exaggerated and pursued until pleasant demeanor became conversation, instead of walking for the principal purpose of showing the dress, the modeling would be defeated; the process would be dillydallying or wasting time.

In the third instance, the principal norm is the pattern of graceful movement, dictated by the desire to move precisely and gracefully. If a subordinate norm, that of leaning far to the left (which is momentarily fitting and answers the exigency of the dance at one point) usurps the principal norm, which is unusually subtle and complex in this case, and the dancer too frequently takes this posture, monotony and impoverishment of effect ensue.

The subordinate norms have extraneous sanctions: the walking on two feet and the watching where she is going, though foreign to the urgent moment of saving her life, is proper for normal traveling. The pleasant conversation, extraneous to the showing of the dress, has sanctions of civilized social behavior. The more than momentary leaning, although it outlasts its moment of fitness and no longer serves the originality and subtlety necessary for graceful performance, when mistakenly prolonged is done so in deference to an esthetic value it had originally.

In artistic form, subordinate norms must declare themselves in the process governed by the principal norm and not be inoperative. The relative poverty of subordinate norms characterizes the objective structure of some paintings of Mondrian, for example, and the viewer resorts to extension of the principal norm either into the subjective or to the transcendent to save the works from vacancy or simplicity. However, once a subordinate norm has been sufficiently expressed to specify the structure, additional function of the same norm becomes superfluity, affectation, or, if it is a qualitative norm, perhaps sentimentality. For instance, the taste of many readers finds excessive the alliteration, rhyme, the stanzaic series, and the trailing alexandrines in Spenser's *Faerie Queene*.

Subordination or hierarchy must be maintained not only among the elements of a structure but also among the substructures. The structural import of the interrelation of substructures is always greater than that of the interrelation of single elements. The ratio of torso to head and of these to the legs of the statue is of greater esthetic consequence than the ratio of one eye to another or that of eyes to nose of the same statue. Accordingly, there is hierarchy of norms in processes. The subordinate norms that serve the principal one of haste in escaping from the flames (crawling under obstructions, beating one's way blindly) are more consequential than others (care of clothing, for example). In the work of art, "the aesthetic norms will delegate the others."[86]

And within the category of the esthetic, whichever precise esthetic effect has managed to become actual (grace, beauty, sublimity, the tragic, majesty, the comic, irony) has priority. Where several effects are suffused, the principal determinant is specified by the effect of that actual expression that in the end is found to have sustained the most acute hazard. The hazards are subordinate though sparring norms, which specify the precise esthetic structure. The "faint half blush that dies along her cheek" that Fra Pandolph found difficult to paint in Browning's "My Last Duchess" is exquisite because the redness, although it is gradually dominated, "dies" only with reluctance. It specifies the portrait, although it has not won its own hazard; it constituted a hazard for the principal norm of whiteness. Again, a circle or curved line exemplifies the specification of a principal norm (centripetalness, curvature) by a series of three hundred sixty subordinate but effectual norms (linear), each operating individually for its own expression at its own particular tangent.

Because hazards are in turn discoverable by their being overcome, advance generalizations seem unwise. For instance, we are told, "a tendency towards the abstract belongs to the essence of linear expression. . . . The purer the artist's work (i.e., the more he stresses the formal elements on which linear expression is based), "the less well equipped he is for the realistic rendering of visible things."[87] Such statements tend (at least) to limit art to expressing explicit norms. The fact is that modes other than the linear are abstractable, too. To make a painting that shows linear expression should not render the artist "less well equipped" for "realistic rendering of visible things," except insofar as he may get out of practice or dim his perception of the visible forms around him. In fact, if in the organization the principal norm is always exclusive abstractive, painting may have to be reclassified as design, which has its own values, it is true, but values proper to a different art.

Dryden, with almost inane simplicity, wrote in "A Parallel of Poetry and Painting":

> To avoid absurdities and incongruities, is the same law established for both arts. The painter is not to paint a cloud at the bottom of a picture, but in the uppermost parts, nor the poet to place what is proper to the end or middle, in the beginning of a poem. I might enlarge on this; but there are few poets or painters who can be supposed to sin so grossly against the laws of nature and of art.[88]

His assumptions are worthy of note: poetry and painting both follow a law or norm of fitness, to avoid absurdity; it is an established norm, and to violate it is to "sin grossly"; it is a norm which is followed not only by the arts of poetry and painting but by nature outside the poem or the painting; poets and painters can be supposed to take the norm of fitness for granted. It is the result of the intelligence we expect to find in poets and painters, who have been in the same world (nature).

Clearly, for Dryden, fitness is high in the hierarchy of norms. What is fit to what is the question, and Dryden gives two examples of what is *not* fit. The painting includes a part which is sky, a part not at the bottom of the picture; thus, the bottom of the picture must be land or water, the only alternatives. And the painter "is not to

paint a cloud" in the middle of the land or water, an
unfit place, but in the sky, a fit place. Something is already given by the assembly of parts of the partially completed painting, namely, the two places (sky and land or
water), and something is to be added by the painter (the
cloud). The fitness is between what is yet to be added and
what is already begun. There is a reason that the cloud is
unfit in the middle of the land or water and fit in the sky,
namely, that a cloud never does exist in the middle of the
land or water in the world of nature outside the painting
and could not since two physical bodies cannot occupy
the same space at the same time. This reason has two
norms involved in it: one is the physical norm, the physical law of the nature of clouds, land or water, and space,
and the other is the norm of the always with clouds, as it
is accepted by the minds of poets, painters, and all who
read poems and see paintings; it is the basis of the norm
of expectancy.

As in physical nature there are "properties," there is
in the mind an expectancy based upon nature to which
one is accustomed. It is the nature of the mind to make
connections between things, or, as Aristotle says, to "gather
the meaning of things." The basis of expectancy is provided by what is already given, the sky and the land or
water, of which the mind grasps the meaning (recognizes
what it represents). The elements already assembled have
cohered to form the basis of meaning ("This is the sky,
and this is the land, and this line is the horizon"). If shiny
things on the land are brightly highlighted and shadows
are very sharply distinct, it would be an error against fitness to put the cloud in the sky, at least in such a way as
to represent the obscuring of the sun, for brightness and
sharply etched shadows "mean" that the sun is shining.
Expectancy registers from the apprehension of meaning,
and if what is given (brightness and sharp shadows) is not
fit to what is added (a cloud over the sun), the painter
has "sinned grossly." The fitness is to be between the
parts or aspects of the painting, and the reason is that as

soon as the parts already assembled have fitness, they have a "meaning," and the meaning is what the other parts must be made to fit. The demand for this is made as expectancy in the mind, for meaning is registered as actual in the mind, and the mind is where the norms of the always or the norms of the must in nature are properly located. Norms are simply the mind's formulation of what it discovers about nature. Dryden's remarks assume the desirability of fitness between the part (to be added) and the part (already there) of the painting and between the norm of fitness in the painting and the norm of the nature of what is referred to by it (the cloud in nature belongs in the sky).

However, in modern painting where the cloud is in the water and the fish in the sky, the second fitness assumed by Dryden is not the norm. Other norms have been substituted. Again, in modern criticism, orientations of interest have been unusually specific, the reference of a novel being viewed, for instance, for a unified spatial apprehension, or that of poetry for the value of a philosophical aspect.[89] Examples could be multiplied, because as soon as elements cohere, the implications of a system begin to cluster, and systems can orient interest to themselves. Each system or substructure has its own intrinsic untouchable status in the total structure, however elusive and mercurial it may be.

But the principle of unity of an artistic form is a key to its value, and until unity is seen, criticism of the work flounders. It is not always easy, in a new genre, for example, to indentify the principle. In my opinion, the poetry of Theocritus has never been given the attention warranted by its value because critics have apparently looked for unity in the composition of such elements as persons and things referred to and thus have emphasized aspects that, in his works, appear trivial. When Theocritus was alive, the esthetic of the graceful was popular, and, like other poets of his day, Theocritus sought it in ways which the Alexandrians were well acquainted with; the

principle of unity in his idyls is the gradual distillation of
grace, a subtle achievement.

In our day, James Joyce's work presents an example of
a shift in the principle of organization. Harry Levin has
shown that Bloom's mind is not a photographic plate, but
a "motion picture, which has been ingeniously cut and
carefully edited." Levin notices a technique of inclusion
and arrangement that gives a clue by which to trace the
principle of unity, namely, "to emphasize the close-ups
and fade-outs of flickering emotion, the angles of observation and the flashbacks of reminiscence."[90] The unifying
principle is perceived in an effect of uninterruptedness.
Conversely, Delmore Schwartz observes of Dos Passos's
USA, "No reader can go from page one to page 1149
without feeling that the newsreels, camera eyes, and biog-
raphies, however good in themselves, are interruptions
which thwart his interest and break the novel into many
isolated parts." And what emerges is not "a novel, but
rather an anthology of long stories and prose poems."[91]
What the unifying principle contributes is intelligibility.
And, contrariwise, as Harold Osborne says, "Any work of
art which is loosely organized is intrinsically indefinite."[92]

ORGANICITY

Although an artistic form is not literally an organism,
it is demanded of form that it be so effectually integrated
as to seem "organic." The distinction that Coleridge made
between mechanical and organic form was a rejection of
the first and an approval of the second. And recently the
distaste for the purely mechanical has carried over even
into arts, where the physical stability of the material of
which the form is made seems in itself to dictate, to use
Coleridge's words, the "impressing of a predetermined
form . . . as when to a mass of wet clay we give whatever
shape we wish it to retain when hardened."[93] An example
of such an art is architecture. Steel, concrete, or marble,

being fixed and unyielding, have physical stability and permanence, and the form imposed upon them traditionally was characterized by an esthetic analogous to stability and permanence, one of balance or mutual assertion through contrast; its macro-structural organization was based upon opposition and similarity. The Greek temple, organized of horizontals, verticals, and diagonals, is an example. It had organic form and its own grace. In contrast, some modern buildings attempt organic form in stone by suggesting the esthetic of the yielding and unstable, analogous to the rise and fall of waves, the curl of smoke, or the posture of a petal. Relationships in the new organic architecture are like those Hiler describes as proper to structuralist design: they are "sequential . . . rather than those of opposition, regarding the . . . configuration as a continuum. These . . . proportionally resemble those found in natural growth."[94]

Conversely, painting, which traditionally exploited the power of pigment to explore infinitesimal variations of color, light, shadow, and spatial complexity, has in modern times adopted strictures proper to concrete and steel, in Cubism. In modern architecture, inorganic matter is informed by structure which imitates the structures of organic matter, and in Cubism, matter with flexibility that easily lends itself to semblance of organic structure is imitating the inorganic, so that form in painting suggests something like (as well as unlike) the form of the Greek temple.

In both the new architecture and Cubism in painting, form resists the potencies of matter; and because the viewer's intuitive assumption of the potentialities of matter is relatively secure, the formal structure is felt as a novelty, novelty founded upon more than the accidental fact that it is new. Moreover, being felt radically as novelty, it is noticeable for its manner. Such propensity to induce awareness has two possible results, depending upon the relation of the matter and form to the final cause or function of the object. The noticeableness of the manner makes demands upon the viewer's attention. If the function of the object is to be esthetically valuable, to induce contemplation of itself, noticeableness is a virtue. In sculpture, for instance, by which traditionally the softness of human flesh is rendered in stone, the noticeableness is not in opposition to its function, form and function being identical. It exists simply to be this particular way. Modern taste tends to be intolerant of traditional sculpture that achieves semblance of softness of garments and flesh, preferring to find the materials showing resistance. Taste, of course, is more fickle than the ratio of matter and form to final cause which constitutes the nature of the work. Consequently, if a great artist arose at present and synthesized the values exploited by modern art and those sought by the art of the past, modern taste would undergo mutation almost over night, a phenomenon often repeated in history.

The potentialities of the matter to be impressed by the form are effectual in aiding the full esthetic result. Where the imposition of form is difficult, as it is on stone informed as soft flesh, the art is taxed, and the difficulty is retrospectively registered and measured against the achievement, with resulting delight (assuming freedom from other obstacles that can interpose, such as sentimentality, triviality, a prevailing fashion of taste). It is a hazard overcome. This is proper enough, since to linger and enjoy the sculptured object is proper.

However, when the function of the object is not simply to induce contemplation of its organization, but something opposed to this, such as utility—the sheltering of the people at worship, the holding all of them securely in one place—the result is different. The principle of utility can have an urgency which gives it precedence in attention over other functions. In the esthetically beautiful building, where people are held securely by the floors and effectually sheltered, the beauty is enjoyed and savored. If the building is unusually beautiful but its floors are known to crack and the roof and walls to be insecure, the beauty is not fully enjoyed. The need for security is a universal and fundamental instinct.

Moreover, in a secure firm building of which the form has a semblance of being soft and yielding, since softness and yieldingness are not virtues proper to the function of the building, the form is experienced as characterized by affectation. The fundamental unity of the nature of the object is disturbed, since formal and final causes appear separated. This is not hazard in the form, that of formal tension. The tension is not felt to be between demands on our attention by both beauty and security, but between the desire for security and the threat of insecurity. It might be objected that purpose and form are not separated if the building which looks insecure is firm in reality. But organic integratedness is properly to be achieved in the semblance to the receiver. It is esthetically irrelevant that a building with dipping and curving walls is in reality not insecure.

Why, then, do we gradually find modern buildings in this style tolerable and before long begin even to like them and to look for them? We begin to put faith in the strength of steel and the miracles of modern technology, then to grow accustomed to them so that insecurity is completely removed, and our esthetic interest becomes free and adventurous.

If that were not so, and insecurity persisted, then, lacking fundamental unity (due to the usurpation by the esthetic principle of the natural priority of the utility principle) this particular type of architectural experiment would not even be organic. Imitating the accidents (curves) of organic matter is not in itself fulfilling the requirement of organic form. True, this style of architecture achieves a dynamism of structure, esthetic disequilibrium. The Greek temple, too, had its indigenous dynamism of structure. Perspective is by its nature dynamic.

Esthetic disequilibrium is not the same thing as formal disequilibrium. Formal equilibrium is assumed; its absence would be imbalance between what is naturally due (fit) and what is achieved. It would result in incompleteness, disunity, or chaos. But the graceful and the sublime (unlike the beautiful) exemplify esthetic disequilibrium, while they characterize formally perfect structure. Disequilibrium does not properly reside exclusively in the organization of the elements of an object, but in the ratio between the power of the object to occasion the receiver's expectancy and the fulfillment of expectancy in actuality.

When Coleridge made the distinction between the machine and the plant to applaud organic form, his expatiating on the idea of the form's developing as if without the agency of the poet was really digressive. Although this was the part taken up by so many critics, the more important idea, initiated before the appositional clause about wet clay, was that of unity. The machine and the plant do not differ on the basis that the form of the first is imposed by the mind and the form of the second is not. They differ in the degree of felt unity. The difference appears in the kind and the manner of the interrelationships of their elements. Whereas the plant and the poem progress in a constantly changing interrelationship of elements, the machine's elements or parts have fixed interrelationship. Whereas the plant's elements are united infinitesimally and invisibly (hence, delicately, hazardously), and the poem's elements are united subtly, and their semblance is temporally (thus fleetingly) rendered, the machine's elements are united in both visible and fixed connections.

In reality the machine has unity, but what is fixed and visible in its connections is unhazardous. In the poem and the plant, the greater the felt obstacles to interrelation, the more we are affected by the glimpse of interrelation when it occurs. In literary meaning, the tightness of unity, which seems cognitively apprehended to be organic, is really an "illusion arising from . . . reaction to hazard. What might appear to be cognitive apprehension is affective impulse at the instant interrelationships are glimpsed."[95] A form is organic when the fitnesses underlying the unity are felt to be triumphs over multiple and various hazards. The receiver's experience of the unity is dynamic, that is, he continues increasingly to discover coherence and to find each fulfillment an absolute.

COMPLEXITY

Since the fitnesses that underlie unity in organic form are triumphs over multiple and various hazards, hazard is indispensable. Any beautiful form in nature or in art must be hazardously integrated. Hazard is central to esthetic value. The elements which tend to frustrate positive relation in formal structure are as important as relationship. Pope, satirizing a formal garden that lacks subtlety, says:

His gardens next your admiration call,
On every side you look, behold the wall!
No pleasing intricacies intervene,
No artful wildness to perplex the scene:
Grove nods at grove, each alley has a brother
And half the platform just reflects the other.[96]

The primitive, too, is lacking in hazard sometimes, and sophisticated taste, desirous of subtlety, scans primitive art, exploring profound relationships. However, these are not always in the object itself but in shadowy corridors of time or tenuous contact with the mute human mind that once applied itself to making the object. These relationships are extrinsic, anthropological, and psychological. They have, though, the charm of mystery, a charm amenable to art. It could be that excessive or exclusive devotion to the primitive in art is rooted in theoretical confusion. But it is a frequent experience to find bewitching depths in primitive art, odd and refreshing appearances and potencies inherent in the structure, and once a deep response is stirred in a person, criticism loses captiousness. Nevertheless, the preoccupation with the "art" of the first grader and the simultaneous neglect of that of Leonardo because the latter had perspective is questionable. The shift in taste, which is revealed in the repudiation of perspective, and the artist's recent piety and respect primarily for the canvas are a change of the field of hazard, a change which could issue ultimately in a new classification, a new kind of art, and possibly, depending on its aim, a different human process from art. But meanwhile, one senses a reduction of the hazards of formal potency.

Moreover, only the actual, says Thomas Aquinas,

> can perfect the potential; and actuality is not, as such, contrary to potency; indeed the two are really similar, for potency is nothing but a certain relationship to act. And without this likeness there would be no necessary correspondence between this act and this potency. Hence potency in this sense is not actualized from contrary to contrary, but rather from like to like, in the sense that the potency resembles its act.[97]

In other words, the potency to carry a tune does not issue in the act of scraping one's foot, because the relationship between the potency and the act it issues in is one of necessary correspondence. When a person has heard the rhythm one-two-three, one-two-three, and the next one-two occurs, the occurrence of three is next if the potency naturally occasioned by the foregone is to have its actuality.

When, on the contrary, it is annihilated by the usurpation of another kind of occurrence, or again, if John cannot carry a tune after all, so that expectancy is frustrated, inference is instantly drawn that the mind was mistaken in some way about the potency, and it waits suspended or sets about making trial of another. In so doing, it gives unconscious affirmation to the enunciated principle of necessary correspondence between "this act and this potency": when one (act) is discovered to be different from what was expected, so must the other (potency) have been. The correspondence is, in fact, the basis of the ancient principle of fitness. Moreover, the more uniquely embedded in the particularity of circumstance, that is, the less corroborated the expectancy and thus the more hazardous, the more exquisite the issuance in act. The Greeks were acutely aware of the fact. Subsequent historical developments, moreover, give new importance to the two aspects of the principle that they did not find it needful to isolate or emphasize.

One is the fact that the correspondence of a potency and its act is necessary and not arbitrary or contingent, so that fitness is grounded in the nature of things. The other, which seems at first to contradict this, is that the mind is essentially engaged with the potency and act of form; it is the mind that registers potency.

This is true of form as a whole and of the dynamic experiencing of a form. Chesterton says, "All my life I have loved frames and limits; and I will maintain that the largest wilderness looks larger seen through a window."[98] The punctual presence of the actual secures it in the mind, and the mind at once explores the correspondent potency (larger . . . largest).

The question frequently raised about the structure of the concrete universal is answerable in these terms. A form that is concrete, unique, unprecedented, is one of which the actualization has been unusual. The mind which apprehends the particularity of an actual particular makes trial of its potency of application to other things by generalizing; and the mind which apprehends the actual universality of a universal, which can exist only in the mind, makes trial of its potency, by making application to a particular. The thing given to the mind and the mind's activity are indispensable and the two interchange, so that given an objective expression of universality, the mind proceeds to particularity, whereas given an objective expression of unique particularity, the mind proceeds to universality.

The fact of the active engagement of the mind with the potencies that have necessary correspondence with actualities in formal structure is corroborated by the findings of Stephen Pepper, who applies a "coherence test" precisely "to find which of the many possible connotative associations arising out of a directly stimulated sensory or perceptual quality are relevant to a work of art." Coherence is established "whenever a connotative expectancy arising out of one directly sensed feature of a work of art is met and reinforced by some complementary connotative expectancy arising from another directly sensed feature of the work. These two expectancies are then said to cohere."[99]

Actually, however, an expectancy is not directly met by an expectancy. When a connotation is apprehended, even though it is not explicit, it is an element of the structure. The fitness experienced is that between a connotation of one sensed feature and that of another. The connotative expectancy may be "met" by another directly sensed feature which instantaneously suggests its connotation. Connotations already registered as such are actual.

Since affective response seems to be greater when the state of potency is prolonged or the act is delayed,[100] it might, being an instance of hazard, seem to present expectancy with more expectancy. But when potency is prolonged and does not come to be actualized in fulfillment, a defeat is felt. Related terms must be actual; relationship between term and term must be occasioned. It is only when, despite hazards of prolonged potency, the "terms" occur as elements of the structure that the illusion of intimate unity is achieved.

A term is "felt" as if it were "met" (to use Pepper's words), as if the actualization occurred with some sort of eager initiative of its own. The eagerness is in the receiver, not in the objective actualization of the term, for that would be impossible. The receiver's cognitive apprehension of the actualization is suffused with affectivity that attends the hazards to its occurrence, and the impulse of affectivity is mistaken as depth of cognition of relationship. The organic unity is felt by the receiver to be inviolable and tight.

This is true no matter how different the arts. Whereas the cognition of poetic form is apprehension of scaffolding, which is partly conceptual because the matter is language and the things signified as images and concepts are actualized along with the sound structure, in music the scaffolding is actualization occasioned only by sound. Accordingly, in poetry affectivity is evoked by hazards in conceptual meaning and by those in actualization of sound patterns, as well as by the coincidence of these, so that affectivity is diffused. In music it is unimpeded by cognitive complexity and is evoked in concentrated intensity.[101]

However, in any formal process or product, when relationship just about triumphs over hazards (acts terminate potencies), relationship is fragile and evanescent. The status of each term is felt to be threatened until the term occurs.[102] This, it seems to me, is why connotation can seem to be only expectancy.

A crude diagram of the elements of any occurrence of relationship would show simply (from the perspective of the receiver whose mind apprehends the relationship):

Term A referring to something, B } all the hazards or obstacles to their relationship { Term B referred to by something, A

The crudeness of this diagram is reflected in the definiteness and stability of the terms and of the obstacles. And of course obstacles are not always spatial, as diagramming suggests they are. Also, the diagram fails to show that any pull upon A by something in the "direction opposite" to B, or upon B by something in the direction opposite to A, militates against the union of A and B; hazards exist elsewhere than in the middle area. At present we are noticing hazard in the status of a term. For instance, the metaphor in *The Rime of the Ancient Mariner,*

And now the storm-blast came, and he
Was tyrannous and strong;

He struck with his o'ertaking wing
And chased us south along!

makes a relationship between a violent wind and a giant
bird of prey. The hazard between them is constituted by
the fact that a storm can never become a bird, nor can a
bird ever be a storm. They are separated by their natures.
The link of their reference is the word *wing*, suggesting a
bird, and other links are that of *blast* with *struck*, signifying violence of each, *tyrannous* and *strong* with *o'ertaking*
and *chased*, connoting hostility, cruelty, and force.

There is hazard in the fragility of reference, though,
owing to the dependence of the whole thing upon the
single word *wing*, the only clue to the fact that it is a
bird which is being related to the storm. The singleness of
wing, as a linking of the metaphor tends to be an obstacle
or condition militating against the relationship of the
terms. It makes the bird shadowy, and we almost failed to
notice it. So when we did, the metaphor was found "interesting"; there was a slight seasoning of affectivity, the
result of which was a renewal of alertness in us. As Susanne
Langer would say, "It liberated perception."[103] In this case,
as in that of any evanescent visual image, fragile and
qualitatively subtle, one experiences the almost-surrender
of term to hazard.

But the *term* must be all but failing; it cannot be
simply hazard somehow hovering. When Coleridge uses
the word *wing*, although the word itself connotes elusive-
ness and departure, the word, instead of fading, begins
more and more to allure the reader's notice, while more
and more hazard accrues; the mind reaches out, loving the
word increasingly, noticing how *o'ertaking* delays its occurrence and suggests the fierce power of the storm which
reaches ahead of the ship; how the battering of the sail in
the sounds of *tyrannous*, *strong*, *struck* gives way to a roar
of the wind in *o'ertaking*, and suddenly *wing* is found faint
in sound; this transfers the whole violent noisy business to
the world of spirits, the invisible beings hurling the ship

forward from under the keel. The ship's plight is felt, too, in the headlong catapulting implied by the sprawling of the word *along*, for instead of the neater "chased us along south," the poet has said "chased us south along." Both prosodically and phonemically the sound *along* suggests an earlier reference to the ship's path trailing in the water: "the furrow followed free."

The more hazardous the term, the more it means and continues to generate meanings. What this amounts to is that being almost not apprehended initially (being subtle), the term's occurring excites affectivity which stirs the mind to alertness, and so in spite of nearly prohibitive subtlety, still more relationship is discovered.

If terms are not subtle but clear and plain, without hazard, then the possible consequents have a high degree of probability. In language such terms would be those of the scientific prose treatise, which in addition to being organized logically, uses words of maximum denotation and minimum connotation, as was mentioned previously; and poetic language (as such, although poetry even of the best does not necessarily use poetic language), in structure only incidentally logical, uses words of maximum connotation and minimum denotation. Poetic language itself, and especially poetic form, has "high entropy," or affective hazard. It is more affective than prose, perhaps less so than music.

The individual word is acutely experienced in the form that has esthetic value, such value being discoverable in the form not as a superficial clothing but present because it is this form, formed this way.[104] A form made of language has more meaning and different meaning than the sum of its elements. It is different meaning, because whereas the sum of its parts simply as such lacks the principle of organization, a particular hierarchization of parts makes it not only one thing instead of many, but this thing rather than that. It has more meaning, because whereas the sum of uncoordinated parts would be a cluster of parts impeded by meaningless juxtapositions, form is constituted by relationships, the foundation of significance. Hierarchization creates and emphasizes relationships. The position of one meaning against another, the posture of tension, occasions more meaning than is made explicit, because the receiver's mind in exploring alternatives finds new relationship, still in the realm of potency. When these are reinforced and confirmed, as they sometimes are, by exploration of alternatives arising from other tensions in the form, potential meanings are moved from the realm of pure potency, somehow closer to actualization by the mind, yet never made explicit.

Moreover, tension is simply the rivalry of distinct relationships (actual or potential) for the mind's attention, and their lure arises from the hazard threatening the terms of each. Eva Schaper observes that a "significant form" is a "fully apparent item," but "significant indicates that the presented and fully apparent form has yet an aspect of unreality about it, for a significant form is an articulated formulation with a potency for signification. It is potentially meaningful, not actually referring."[105] Such radioactivity of meaning could not be occasioned by the mere aggregation of parts.

In plot, dynamic reference, hazards can occur in the pull between what seems caused versus what results. We find them if the feedback is startling: what was expected versus what is realized. Sometimes, too, ironies are delicately made apparent. Occasionally, character depth or some static reference becomes quietly actualized and enlarged in a turn of event. Central and acute hazards frequently threaten probability.

Where reference is not unfolded as a plot but tends in all directions at once amid terms which are viewed as if they had been established previously to the poetic utterance, lyrical stasis is present. And here, too, we can apply words that Meyer used to describe structure in music. For meaning here "is not a static, invariant attribute of a stimulus, but an evolving discovery of attributes."[106] Nothing could more aptly describe response to the increasing intensity of lyrical stasis than "evolving discovery of attributes." The reasons are traceable to dynamic aspects in both sound and meaning of the lyric.

The structure of sound proceeds in time as do both music and the dynamic reference of a story. And the dynamic aspect of static meaning is due to the change from not seeing relationships to seeing, more and more, intensity increasing as meaning possibilities beckon to and elude the mind. Although the meaning is static, as there is no progression in a plot, there is a change in degree of intensity. The newly occurring events in the dynamism of sound structure allure the attention and present hazards to the meaning's hold on the attention; when meaning sustains the hazard, affectivity is felt, and this is experienced as increased intensity of meaning.

In lyrical poetry, moreover, sound sometimes bends meaning to its sway, while meaning continues to widen and deepen, and the mind is exercised in oscillation between their lures. The mind discovers attributes of sound, of meaning, of sound again, and never chooses to relinquish either. It is a miniature tug-of-war between analogs of time (dynamic sound structure) and space (widening out of newly discovered meanings).

Thus, if complexity does not appear in one way, it appears in another. When things are unquestionably beautiful or graceful, the chances are that complexity is present, even though it may be disguised as simplicity, as it is when complexity is qualitative. An example of this is found in the rainbow. Susanne Langer, discussing the terms in a beautiful object in nature, observes: "The most striking visual objects in the natural world are optical—perfectly visible 'things' that prove to be intangible, such as rainbows and mirages."[107] This is true.

A great part of the charm of the rainbow is in its being so richly and exquisitely dyed *at the same time* that nothing is in fact there: an airplane could go right through it. The italicized words suggest that there is a ratio upon which such charm depends: the relationship between the appearance of something and the known presence of relatively nothing. To be enchanted by that, one must both see the appearance and know about the nothingness. The usual state of affairs is that when there is an appearance, there is something in which it inheres; it is the appearance of something. The rainbow represents a delightful deviation from that norm, and deviation is a hazard, the norm being one term, the edge of deviation being the other, and the extent of the difference being the hazard.

But that is not the rainbow's only or its deepest charm. The fact is that the whole sky is empty of rainbows; that when one appears, it is an appearance of something that is not in the empty sky most of the time. It has the numerical hazard of the rare. And it is not a great strip of ribbon or of marble. The material is fragile and barely able to cohere. The existence of the terms is threatened. This is subtle hazard in itself, and it is what the delighted gazer keeps exploring in his imagination. He is more sophisticated than the child, knowing the scientific explanation for the rainbow. But he thinks nevertheless that its existence is a sort of minor miracle.

However, there is more to the rainbow's charm than that. If it came after much blandishment and coaxing, such as so delicate a miracle might be expected to require, it would be enjoyable enough. But there it is without agency, and it takes us by surprise, when we were well habituated to gloom. This is a hazard of act, absolved of the labor of potency.

It has, moreover, an irritating temporal hazard. The eyes keep seeking it and holding it, knowing it will fade in a minute. Every second of its existence is hazardous and thus has its role in adding to the affective experience.

Perception is, under the affective stimulus, liberated and wide awake. And the infinitesimal bewildering hazards of the spectrum are threatening the fragile occurrences all along the infinitely graduated scale from saturation to saturation, never once repeating a hue, every new modification attracting notice. It is endless variety in unity, and the attention oscillates between the all-colors-as-one-striped-band phenomenon and the lure of qualitative hazard where one color is less itself than a melting into the other.

The brilliant perfection of the arc is infinite, tangential variety in unity, and the degree of its precision is felt as a victory over all the imperfections of the usual.

And the rainbow is of no use. It has the status hazard of the nonuseful, contributing to its splendor. It is pure celebration.

Moreover, even the lining up of nine kinds of hazard does not account with completeness for the esthetic effect as it is in reality experienced. In talking about it, one necessarily deals with it as a generality. But every rainbow occurs uniquely, and every subtle microscopic grading of the variety it presents is a winsome particular, most hazardous in itself.

Susanne Langer, in seeing the "semblance" or "image" of every art object as if it were a rainbow, shows sensitiveness to this enchantment. Of course, those things that are not the rainbow do not renounce the power of charming by their embeddedness in material reality; even though there cannot be an omnipresent rainbow, there are omnipresent hazards, always incarnated in new appearances. The rapidity of intuition and of the mind's oscillation and the hold of hazardous structure on the will engages the whole person. Perception of the part, and another part, instantly becomes the grasp of the whole gestalt, and then a new savoring of the part, etc., in rapid and prolonged alternation. The experience is a totality (determined by the object), and the totality is interrelationship. It is so acute an experience that its reality is astonishingly established.

In the complexity of some abstract modern paintings that one estimates to be genuinely successful, the oscillation is among beautiful fragments so alluring that attention reaches to hold them all at once, whereas their mutual exclusion militates against it, and they elude unity. The spectator is "exercised" by them; one feels that the adventurous reaches of the paintings will be a gain to painters in the future, but as long as wholeness is lacking, they assume the character of brilliant exercises.

The complexity of a finished form, its "difficulty,"[108] is akin to its privilege and autonomy. Its value is clearly not utility. And its value is not identical with its meaning. Vivas, in a paragraph about meaning in Lawrence's work, might give that impression when he says that only "at the level of mere apprehension" and not of "experience . . . addressed to practical ends . . . an object can become fully significant, meaningful."[109]

In response to both the esthetic object and a practical result desired, there is "grasp" of significance. Moreover, the meaningfulness attachable to "mere apprehension" can be found in both cases, even though, as Vivas indicates, there is a difference between responses proper to each of the two.

In the first case, that of "grasp of a thing as significant" and "addressed to . . . practical ends," the finding of the relationship can be crucial, for example, the answer to a mathematical problem for estimating the distance of an enemy target. The answer might be connected with the possibility of reaching the target, therefore winning the battle, thereby turning the tide of the war, thereby terminating it with all the conditions attached thereto and their effect on history. Nevertheless, hundreds of people engaged in bringing about this development might be doing a small part of the whole and not recognize the "significance" of their duties. The boy who solves the initial mathematical problem of the measurement of the distance might not know the full significance of his answer. To realize it, he would have to know these relationships: (1) the right answer, to the question, (2) the application of the answer, to a correct discharge of the ballistic missile, (3) the danger from the enemy, to the threat of destruction of the enemy by the missile, (4) the resolve of the enemy, to the threat of destruction, (5) the resolve of the nation, to the resolve of the enemy, (6) the ending of the war, to these resolves, (7) the signing of the treaty, to the ending of the war, (8) the developments of history, to the signing of the treaty. The mental surveying of these relationships is "mere apprehension." What Vivas says is true, that by apprehension the whole thing "can become fully significant." The significance, that is, the relatedness, is seen. But the distinction is not that between the practical and the nonpractical; it is between surveying of relationships and not doing so.

However, where a practical end is visible, and especially when the need for it is urgent, the mind does not dwell on relationship as such. It passes over this in its direct reach for the end, becoming unaware of the steps in the relationship. In artistic form, however, the mind is engaged totally with the interrelationship of aspects. Mutual reference unifies the structure, overcoming the centrifugal lure of reference of reality outside it. The mind more than half relinquishes reality outside it, giving itself to the contemplation of relationship in the structure, noticing the various facets of it. In so doing, the mind sees facets as themselves, not as signs of other things.

Thus, in the case of the mathematical solution that changes history, the Secretary of War would see it in a way quite different from the poet. The secretary would exploit its use, and the poet its paradoxes and the ironies of the connection between so small a cause and so large an effect.

Indeed, one of the reasons why the poet's engagement with the magnitude of the fields of relationship is felt to issue in something fully significant is that the urgency of winning the war, of reaching the target therefore, therefore of solving the mathematical problem *is* so practical a matter. The surveying of universal urgencies from an all-viewing vantage gives the poet a tone of godlike proprietorship. High-handedness is felt in his advertence to relationship as such in the presence of the practical as well as of the multitudes included by the poet's glance. Reality and the urgencies of the practical thus bring hazards to the mutuality of reference in the structure, and the success of the poet in achieving the vast, difficult unity is responded to by the mind's awareness. The mind oscillates in its increasing cognitive attention to relation, in the excitement of assimilation of hazard. The presented hazard to relationship within the structure itself, the complexity taxing unity to the utmost, heightens awareness.

The reasons why this can be satisfying are that powers of the whole mind are exercised, unable to exhaust the implications; that the practical aspects are seen as such but transformed, because it is their significance or importance that is celebrated. The aspects are vested with a superior life, that of meaning, beyond that of brute fact. The unity of meaning is experienced as composure, too. Even when the stimulus of hazardous form impels the mind to reach to designated extra-poetic realities, the congruences in the structure affirm the fundamental equilibrium of the meaning. Actually, the mind cannot resist seeking relationship when hazards attend it and cannot separate its attention from relationship once it is found. The form, which is a system of remote and vast congruities in intricate proportion, lures the mind back. Contemplation is what the human mind was created for; the poem is "humanizing." Human beings are more human as they are more aware, and form occasions intensity of awareness by incarnating value.[110]

Value

Many times in the course of a day a person experiences a requirement or attraction, for one reason or another, to something not quite obtained. Around mealtime, it is the requirement of the body for food; in the stalled automobile, it is the need of the engine for gasoline; in the state of uncertainty about some arrangement, it is the want of someone or something to explain it; in the middle of listening to a joke, it is the punch line. The wished-for thing is invested with some "value," which borrows its character partly from the nature of the wish. In the cited examples these would be, respectively, food value, power value, communication value, comic suspense value. Moreover, the wished-for thing can satisfy the wish only if it has a certain "virtue,"[111] which in the above instances would be vitamins, combustibility, clarity, wit. If the food is spoiled, or the gasoline diluted, the letter in an unknown language, and the joke garbled, the wished-for thing does not satisfy. It lacks its own proper virtue.

To insure to a thing its own virtue, some principle must direct its manner of existence, by which it is this kind of food rather than that, or whereby it is a certain combination of elements in the gasoline which renders it combustible, or certain written signs in the communication which represent intelligible words intelligibly arranged, or whereby elements of the comic incident are withheld until the precise moment when their release is desirable. The principle is a guide of choice of what will best fulfill the requirement and of avoidance of what will obstruct fulfillment. It issues from consciousness of the need. The thing satisfying the requirement is always in itself some organizedness—chemical, linguistic, logical, psychological —and the principle is the way it is best organized for satisfying the requirement. The principle of organization is the means of the virtue, and the virtue is the means of the value.

In a poem or any work of fine art, the means and end of the work are found identical, the principles or norms of process appear as structure in the product,[112] and the structure itself actualizes the value. The value is always unique and particular. This fact has so impressed many students of literature that they have condemned any generalization or theory of esthetic, confusing the knowledge of what value is, and what in the work occasions it, with the response to the particular value. Even though the organization of each poem is necessarily unique, the concepts and terminology supplied by theory are tools to enable us to know it better. Even without the stable terminology indispensable to the best condition for criticism, awareness that results from increasing concern with evaluation constantly finds expression in various ways.

Thus, Dorothy Van Ghent compares the structure of *Clarissa* to a circle and that of *Tom Jones* to a Palladian palace. Or she observes parallelism in the impervious character of Madame Merle and Gilbert Osmond, on the one hand, and the caricature of imperviousness in Henrietta Stackpole, on the other.[113] Tillotson, describing Pope's rhyming, says his "couplets are not all equally prominent . . . A couplet of Pope's is like a range of hills with rises and falls, with sometimes a plateau in prominence, sometimes a peak."[114] Stallman notices that Crane's "The Open Boat" is "constructed of alternating moods, each built-up mood of hope . . . being canceled out by contradictory moods."[115]

From such passages as these, about particular virtues of particular works, we see clearly that critics are busy about organization principles in artistic forms. In the absence of established terminology, they are employing similes, metaphors, and words that approximate literary effects. In each instance, although the critic is describing a particular, there is reference to something generic to characterize the principle: the circle, the Palladian palace, a parallel, rises and falls, alternation. In every case, too, the reference clarifies the work a little more for the reader by describing in a general way the principle of its structural value.

The question of what value is and the "perplexing problem of value and value theory" must be faced in spite of "many heated discussions raging in these areas."[116] The sound and fury continue because value is difficult in itself, and its importance has been obscured for years.

Whatever value may be, it is always constituted by relation.[117] The kinds of value, moreover, are distinguishable one from the other, even when, as often happens, several values characterize the same object and are interrelated in it. The monetary value of a quarter is constituted by its exchangeability for bread and its being part of a money system. The linguistic value of a word is constituted by its referring to an idea and its inclusion in a language system.[118] The philosophical value of an insight is constituted by the difference of degree of its penetration and that of the hitherto most penetrating insight, on the one hand, and its consistency with the system of known philosophy, on the other. The moral value of an action is constituted by its unprecedentness and the extenuation of its circumstances and its adherence to the system of the moral law. The scientific value of a hypothesis is constituted by its reach and the area of unproved knowledge included by and dependent upon it and its likelihood in relation to

known scientific laws and facts. The scientific value of a
fact is constituted by its clarity and distinctness from all
else and by the strength of systematic proof and the
scope of its implications.

Value, in short, always includes an element of uniqueness, differentness, or exchangeability but also a relatedness to a system. And in every instance of value, the
system identifies the value.

To say of a novel that it "has" a psychological value,
for instance, is to refer to two things, namely, the novel
itself and psychology. They are not the same thing. Psychology is a science, and as such it is "systematized conceptual knowledge."[119] Being systematized, it shows order
among its elements, laws of its own. And it has mature
existence before the novel is originated, with complete in-
dependence of it. The same is true of the sciences of
politics, anthropology, ethics, or any other science, and also
of philosophy. These systems have their existence properly
in human minds, being knowledge.

When a philosopher reads a great novel, the chances
are that he will gain a new philosophical insight. This
will happen because the words conjure up in his imagination a whole universe of human lives having philosophical
relevance. His mind is prepared to see philosophical implications of these lives, because he brings to his reading the
preexisting system of his knowledge, which is now seen
in relationship with the concrete unprecedented situations
of characters in the novel. The new insight that he enjoys is experienced as valuable. It is constituted both by
the difference in degree of its penetration from insights
hitherto enjoyed by him and by its striking consistency
with his knowledge. The value emanates from the system
of his philosophy that the fictional situation corroborates
and from the unique purity of the fictional situation as
this issues from the nature of the characters.

The philosopher gets insight from situations in real
life, also. What the novel does with efficiency is to fur-
nish him unusually clear instances, and with an emphasis

which stimulates his proper mental searches beyond their usual intensity.

Philosophers and scientists are not the only people who notice such values in a literary work; any of us might, since philosophy and science have as their materials things which are a part of our lay knowledge and experience. Although in a less complete and planned way than that of the specialist, we may have a "philosophy" or some partially systematized knowledge directly relevant to the things referred to by the literary object. When we read a novel, our minds are engaged with the characters and events, which are concrete and clear and felt with intensity. Undistracted, we notice everything and there is reason for everything, all is eventuated and concluded, all interrelated. In this respect, as in many others, the novel differs from everyday life, in which we see people in the street without following them home and seeing the significance of their getting off *this* bus, or without knowing all that preceded and will follow the few sentences we may have heard them utter. In other words, much of what we witness all day long is "meaningless" because it is fragmentary, not seen in relation to causes and effects and parallels. But in the novel, whatever is there is related to everything else that is there; every character, situation, conversation, even every gesture and word has a reason for being there; that is, it is "related" to other characters, situations, possible eventualities. That is another way of saying that it is meaningful or significant, for meaning is a relation between references. In life, apart from the novel, when a situation or action is seen in relation to its cause, its effects, or its connections with other events, it is seen to be a significant event. The novel gives us a concentration of significant events, and in that sense, as in others, it differs from life where we usually do not and more often cannot trace significance.

When, in the reading of the novel, the mind is attentive to the thoughts, apprehensions, curiosity, words and plans, of a character, one notices the unique situation in which the character is placed and feels his anxieties and all the pressures of circumstances. This is a unique situation into which the character is lured and locked, and the reader's mind is nimbly exercised measuring alternatives, hoping for ways out, turning the whole thing rapidly this way and that as he reads, suspecting what will happen. The reason he can appreciate it so wholly is that he is human, too, and maybe he is a sophisticated reader who can catch the extraordinary fitness of even half-issuing, subtle possibilities to advanced knowledge of the way such a character might behave under those pressures. If the character's psychological extenuation is subtle and intimate and the reader's knowledge of psychology is vast and sure, and if now the two, related automatically in his mind, corroborate each other, something unusual and exciting occurs for the reader. It affects his preexisting knowledge of psychology, his insight into the psychology of the fictional character, his response to the novel as a whole, and to himself.

His knowledge of psychology has enjoyed a sudden intuitive enlargement of boundaries, the sort of opening up of possibilities that the scientist calls hypothetical, penetrating all the leaven of his knowledge which tentatively adjusts to possibilities. At the same time, his insight into the psychology of the fictional character enjoys an instantaneous lengthening into unexplored regions created by the framework of extenuating circumstance. The unprecedented circumstance calls into play latencies in the character, hitherto untried and unexercised. The reader's mind experiences what might be called dilation as it reaches for the suddenly retreating frontier of the hypothetical (in psychology) and the retreating frontier of the fictional human being. The sudden spreading out of the field of possible cognitive relationships is felt as affective hazard. He experiences exhilaration, the accompaniment of a "psychological value."

But in the literary work of art, the character in the unprecedentedness of his own circumstance, seen as the center of a structure or field of psychological interrelationships, the whole field in turn related to other psychological fields or structures, is only one element in the whole structure of the novel. Other elements attract the mind at the same time. If the reader is a sophisticated moralist, and the extenuated moral situation in which a human act is performed by the fictional character gives the act extraordinary specificity, new moral insight stretches the field of the reader's awareness of moral law and at the same time excites his exploration of the act. The effect is experience of moral value. In the same way, for the political theorist and for the sociologist, political values and sociological values might be found to inhere in the universe of meaning called up in the mind by the words of the novel.

The average reader is not a psychologist, moral theologian, political theorist, sociologist, or any other such specialist. But he is, ideally, a mature and intelligent person who has a layman's knowledge of human beings and hence of the elements of these sciences. In fact, even if he *is* a psychologist, his experience of the psychological value in a literary work is not the scientific act of a psychologist. The value is an enjoyable expansion of the mind which, though informed, is temporarily in the attitude of the lay mind surveying relationship, internal distances, among elements that are psychological.

Since relationship is not identity, two elements brought into the relationship of likeness are by that fact isolated by the mind from all in which they have been embedded, all that is not like them. In the relationship which occasions a psychological value (that between the unexplored reach of the psychological insight into a character and the center of the system of psychological science), the elements that are *not* psychological are elements in which the psychological is embedded. The psychological value accords with the laws of psychology; the political value with its own political laws; the moral value with the moral law. All of these systems of psychology, politics, and ethics are foreign to and independent of the structure of the novel. A moral, political, sociological, or psychological

value in a literary object is unmodified by all the reference
in the artistic structure. Each value accords with its own
laws (system), which are foreign to the structure. Therefore, each value keeps its own entity. And yet, since each
becomes part of the conditions in which the unique occasion of the other is made possible, each becomes, so to
speak, a qualification of the others, which would be different without its presence. Moreover, it is in the reader's
mind that values are actualized, value being dependent
upon relation; and since the experience of a value by the
reader suffuses his mind and issues in unusual interest, the
experience of the other value, and then another, is re-
ceived by him in a state of mind that is qualified. In this
sense too, each value becomes a qualification of the other.

Yet, as has been said repeatedly, psychological value
can be found elsewhere than in a literary work and is, in
fact, proper to the science of psychology; and the same
rule applies in all the different sciences and in philosophy.
Moreover, these values when in their proper spheres are
always truth values, although their terms are different
aspects of truth (reality). The psychological value of an
occurrence, when it is a datum of the science of psychology, might not welcome as neighbors political, moral,
and sociological values, which might be irrelevant. The
elements must be psychological, and the systematization
of them must be the basis of the science of psychology; so
too with each of the sciences. In all of these instances,
there are fundamental differences to be seen between
values—psychological, moral, political, sociological—occurring in their own proper spheres and those same values
occurring in the literary work of art.

In the work of art, these values all occur as intermin-
gling substructures of a whole structure so organized as to
occasion esthetic value and to exist for that purpose. Not
that they exist before the esthetic whole, like building
blocks, nor does the esthetic object exist before them.
They co-occur; there are many other values besides
(sound, lexical, grammatical), each occasioned by the

presence at the same time of all. The posture of the combination of all is the extenuating of circumstance in which each is occasioned. The totality is the esthetic system. Esthetic value occurs when one element or cluster of elements of the whole structure is as hazardously deviant from the purpose implied by the structure as it can get without being lost to it. The relationship of its extremity to the center of the structural system is felt as tenuous but successful.

To say an element or cluster of elements is hazardously deviant from the purpose implied by the structure means simply that those elements attract the reader's notice to the point of endangering its re-advertence to the system. They beckon to him, and he would give himself to them were he not presently aware that in their extreme original grace the whole system is confirmed (his mind retaining the system in general which is newly felt as multiplied in value) at the same time that he is teased by the demands made by the graceful deviation upon his notice. The "*discrimen* of the aesthetic . . . is coherence of structure simply as such," and in the receiver the result is "a concern with such coherence."[120] The form as an end in itself is the valuable thing. And the "patterns of order" in it have a bearing upon its "value."[121] Value is perceived when a form is "full, sphere-like, single."[122]

When Dorothy Van Ghent says of *Tess of the D'Urbervilles* that "philosophical vision . . . inheres as the signifying form of a certain concrete body of experience; it is what the experience 'means' because it is what, structurally, the experience is,"[123] she is talking about some kind of value. The body of experience of the characters in the novel means something, and its meaning is the "philosophical vision." She is using the word *vision* not in the sense of power to see, but in the sense of something that is seen. What is seen inheres as the signifying form of the body of experience. Although what a thing *is* cannot be what it *means*, or vice versa, since meaning is relationship between terms that are never identical, her real point is

that "as a structural principle active within the particulars
of the novel . . . the philosophical vision has the unassailable truth of living form." She considers *Tess of the
D'Urbervilles* to have some sort of philosophical value.
Why?

The experiences referred to in the novel are clear. The
reader, in whose mind the "body of experience" takes
shape as meaning structure, perceives it as a unique experience of the people (characters). The reader comes to
the novel with a certain awareness of ultimates (philosophical system) and of the moral law (system of moral-
ity). This is general, transcending particulars. When the
mind discovers the body of unique experience in the
novel somehow to confirm and yet to stretch the applica-
bility of these systems, it sees in the novel philosophical
and moral values. The "philosophical vision" (things
seen) which Van Ghent rightly claims to be inherent in
the experience, is a system, understood ultimate reality,
or perhaps moral law. The unique experience is one thing,
and the system is another. Both are registered in the mind
of the reader, brought together by the reading. Each
acutely and deeply implies the other, and each thus illu-
mines the other. That this is true is corroborated by the
nature of each.

The particulars of the novel she is talking about are
seen as unified by a "structural principle," and the principle is something philosophically grounded. It is a
principle which has some sort of truth, namely the truth
to be found in principles grounded in the significance of
particulars in real life. In life outside of and prescinding
from the novel, there are people who are constituted individually and who, in their circumstances and for their
own motives, perform actions, talk, rejoice, suffer. There
is a continuity in their lives; they do things for reasons
and with more or less remote ends in view, and this has
its consequences. This is another way of saying that to
anyone who might know all, their lives are structured,
and, to a greater or lesser degree, unified. There are rela-

tionships between motive and action, between memory and hope, between deeds and their results. This is what is meant in the expression "living form." When we examine such pattern in lives, and relate them to each other and to ultimate considerations about mankind, we abstract from all the particulars included something true of them all and state it. This is a philosophical principle. Even should we not do this scientifically and meticulously, we tend to do it as we grow older and wiser, as we see pattern in life. This becomes even for the layman in philosophy a sort of wisdom, sometimes systematic as it aligns itself, when principles show consistency and are borne out by more and more proof from life.

In *Tess of the D'Urbervilles*, Van Ghent finds the particulars of the lives of the characters to progress and show pattern, when viewed in the light of such principles. So if one examines the philosophical aspect of the novel, not only does one see structure or internal consistency, but in addition, one sees external consistency, that is, adherence to the same principles one gleans from the philosophical consideration of real life. This shows the novel to have a value which is designated here as "unassailable truth"; truth, because it conforms to principles grounded in reality, and unassailable, because to deny these would be to falsify the experience of life available to everyone. Thus, the novel is a new exemplification of the system popularly known as human wisdom, and at the same time the system has the probability or internal consistency that determines the novel. The novel viewed from that aspect is characterized by philosophical value.

Just as the philosophical vision is a structural principle, so the psychological consistency is another, the anthropological another, each aspect according to which the novel is viewed showing a structure, and all of these being substructures of the whole novel which is an esthetic structure. Esthetic structure is structure per se. Looking at a painting, we might abstract only all the blueness, and then looking at another aspect of it, we might focus only on perspective, the here-to-thereness; and again, the variety of values of black in it. To see these things, we must come to the painting with previous knowledge of what blue is, with previous experience of spatial perspective, and with awareness of values and degrees of black. These are, however, simple generalities, which as such belong to "systems"—each separate from and independent of the painting—systems we would recognize even were we never to have seen this painting. And when we do see it, each value (blueness, perspective, blacknesses) keeps its own identity in the structure of the painting, the blueness never being blackness or perspective, but always remaining itself as blueness for one's notice to advert to. This phenomenon Wilson prizes in a scene of a work of Yeats when he says, "the personal emotions it awakens and the general speculations which these emotions suggest, have been interwoven and made to play upon each other at the same time that they are kept separate and distinct. A complex subject has been treated in the most concentrated form, and yet without confusion."[124]

In the painting, the bluenesses would not be of interest if there were not blacknesses among which they were embedded and contrasted, nor could perspective even appear were there not the bluenesses and blacknesses. Structure as such, esthetic structure, delicate organization occasions the values. In the novel, the psychological matters in which the action is embedded help to occasion the moral value of it; the moral texture in which the social is framed occasions the social value of it; and structure as such provides mutual interaction, embeddedness, "framing" for each of the values. Consequently, frame or limit, or, more accurately, form as internal relationship, constitutes the indispensable and only occasion of value. The novelist's "picture of life" derives its "high value from its form," Henry James says.[125] If the structure is perfect, every element of it gains in potential value. When Maritain says that although a poem "must preserve its . . . unique value as an object, at the same time it is a sign" of "secrets perceived in things," what he is observing is that "things" in the poem seem to take on their own values, which he perceives as "some ineluctable truth in their nature" or some "adventure" that is "transpierced by . . . intuition," as he says, "suddenly."[126] Nevertheless, it is because (not although) the poem preserves its unique value as an object that these sudden adventures are actual.

By repudiating form in art, many a modern artist destroys the only condition which would provide the very thing he seeks. The word *value* is not a word of good repute in his books. Well, then, it is just as accurate to say that when we destroy form, we destroy the possibility of ecstacy, the last extremity and beyond, of response— to the last extremity and beyond, of "value." It can be called universal truth, cosmic grandeur, that which annihilates all speech, or whatever. Warfare among ideologies, and clashes among critics, leave feelings of hostility toward words which thereafter carry derogatory connotations. Such a word is *form*, and another is *value*. They have survived many a polite war, not without losses. It is nevertheless a fact that (1) form as such occasions value; (2) that affectivity attends our contemplation of it, although affectivity as such is not value; (3) that in a poem, a painting, or other artistic work, several values are mingled, and therefore critics who tend to give all attention to one value alone have a distorted vision; (4) that structuralness transforms the nonesthetic values; and (5) that each value constitutes a hazard to the others.

Value and Formal Hazard

The particular condition that makes a form valuable in itself is, we say, esthetic. Esthetic value is a general term. Even within the category of esthetic value, there are various values such as gracefulness, sublimity, majesty. An esthetic value is attributable to things in nature and to objects of art on the same grounds. Where esthetic value in one object differs from esthetic value in another, it is not because one is an art object and the other a natural object. This would be a difference simply of origin.[127] The difference between their esthetic values results from difference between the manner of organization of elements of the one and the manner of organization of elements of the other.

An esthetic value is constituted by relation between a part of the object, on the one hand, and the whole structural system that constitutes the object, on the other. System appears to be everywhere in nature and in the affairs of daily life, as well as in art structures.

If someone idly standing in a doorway which led into a room were to notice on the opposite wall a picture of a girl in a meadow, and to notice the subtle shades, between rose and coral, of her billowing skirt, he would become attentive to the subtleties of color. If presently he noticed that the wallpaper had an alternating pattern in which, at every third unit, a white flower were repeated, of which the upper left petal curled away in a position which invited a light on its surface, and this melted into the same rose shade as that of the skirt of the girl in the picture, his look would be attracted to the rose surfaces, now to this one, now to that, then to the skirt, and to as many of the instances of the flower pattern as he could encompass in his glance. Were the entire wall, the picture frame, and the canvas to be a solid rose color, it would not be interesting. Interest results from the fact that one flower is separated from the other by expanse of wall and by alternating flowers of other patterns, that the oscillating of the attracted notice continues. And the more interesting fact that the skirt is not the flower keeps the notice in a continuous reversion to the skirt. Then, if the observer discovers that the piping on the lampshade is of the same delicate off-rose color, his attention is delightedly teased into exploring the sameness of difficult color in these diverse occurrences; and added to the interest of this is the awareness of deliberate planning behind the arrangement. Abstractly, it might be said that sameness (of color) is found to triumph over differentness (between here, there, flower, wall, skirt, lampshade), and to do so with a certain amount of difficulty (the chances against achieving so subtle a color more than once and the task of holding it all in one glance).

Aware, then, of plan (system), he explores with his eyes, noting that the draperies are gray. But when he sees them in contrast to the pure gray of the carpet, he sees that mixed in the gray of the draperies is a tint of rose. They are gray which is trying to be rose, so to speak, and when he observes this, and sees them in relation to the skirt, petals, and lampshade piping, his attention is held by the desire to keep exploring it. The draperies are seen as tending toward rose and yet not quite achieving it—a hazard to relation—and as tending toward the purity of the gray of the carpet but not quite achieving it. The not-quiteness, which is a condition of potentiality not actualized, is experienced as a condition of being still hidden, a condition describable as subtle. The faint color of rose almost lost in the gray is related to the system of rose color in other parts of the room.

In this simple example, structure is exemplified in the organization of color elements of sameness and difference; and an esthetic quality is exemplified in the subtlety of the organization, in which sameness of rose (unity) is felt to triumph though with difficulty, over difference of gray (variety). The response of the receiver is exemplified as one of absorbed interest in structure (interrelationship) as such, the attention oscillating between elements and groups of elements.

It is true that the structure just described would not excite the viewer to any unusual degree. It would please him in a subdued way. But things in nature or in art which are unusually beautiful, unusually graceful, unusually sublime, and so forth, excite us deeply. Structure is found valuable for its own sake, holding the attention by attraction to its structuralness. The difference between the experience of the color structure of the room and that of structure of an unusually beautiful object is a difference of degree.

Between two objects, both of which have the quality of beauty, that one will be more beautiful which has more complexity controlled by the more successful unity. In other words, it has more of each—complexity and unity. But what this comes to is more complexity; there can be no difference in degree of unity as such. Unity is achieved, or it is not. This is true because unity is interrelatedness, and, as Saint Thomas Aquinas says, "relations cannot be more or less."[128] Nevertheless, the more there is that is interrelated, the more differentness overcome, the more the value of beauty is occasioned. Another way of saying this is that the more subtle the organization of elements, the more beautiful is the structure. Complexity, or variety, does not have to be quantitative; it may be qualitative. In beautiful structure as it is found in nature and in art, it is usually both. But qualitative complexity is less likely to be noticed; it is more subtle.

Thus, enormous variety among a great number of large and far reaching elements, held together in unity, is not necessarily more beautiful than complexity among small immediate elements held together in unity. It is neither the number nor the size of the elements but the complexity, the subtlety of the organization into unity, that determines the degree of value. This is demonstrated in the fact that a Shakesperean sonnet holds the mind as securely as a Shakesperean tragedy or an epic, and the rose and dogwood tree as surely as the firmament.[129] The ratio between complexity and unity in a structure, not between the size of the elements, determines the degree of beauty. Does unity somehow manage to triumph over its own unique obstacles—that is the important question, regardless of scale, since obstacles are not all spatial, temporal, or numerical.

The rose is more beautiful than the room I described, because its complexity is hazardous and subtle in the extreme and its unity absolute. Although the petals are all of the same general structure or shape and are attached at their pointed end, they are graded in size, and each is unique in its position around the center, each tends to its individual posture—some toward the center, some half toward and half away, some away from it, an outermost petal here or there curling at its edge. In this complete variety of posture, the deepness of red rose is gathered near the unfolding around the center; the light softly melts into change of hue as it strikes the gradually less curled petals and tends toward delicate pallor in the outermost petal, which tries to curl outward. This hierarchy and gradation is all held around one center, each petal maintaining its unique place and status of position and color value. The slight curve of the stem, and the climax of alternation among delicate fringed and shining leaves, each postured uniquely but in harmony with the whole spiral, is important and noticeable. Additional im-

portance accrues to the rose from its singleness, its way
of existing simply to be beautiful, from its graceful casual
relation to its stem and to its slender shadow. It gathers
an air of unspoiled exquisiteness, too, from its unagressive
return to senses other than sight—its coolness, softness,
and pure fragrance. These last are not its beauty, but they
accompany and corroborate the experience of pleasure that
necessarily attends our contemplation of beauty. In addition, the beauty of it is accentuated by connotations—
the rare occasion, dignity, expensiveness, graciousness of
manner, bestowal, memorableness. But these last, although they are fitting accompaniment of the experience
of the beauty of the rose, still do not constitute its beauty,
which is restricted in this case to the realm of visual structure. This fact is not always distinct in the account of
estheticians, some of whom confuse beauty with connotative meaning.

Sometimes when two roses are compared, their value
is not estimated to be equal. Occasionally, a viewer is im-
pelled to conclude that one in particular is perfect, exquisite, or, as sometimes happens in the exceeding degree
of the experience of the moment, the most exquisite
thing he has ever seen. This happens if, let us say, a petal
leans away from the subtle manifold, curling away from
the center and down toward the stem, and another, not
directly opposite but slightly to the left of the point directly opposite, and on the upward side of the rose in its
posture, is reaching upward away from the center and
from the stem, blushing deep color at its most exposed
curve of saturation, the qualitative gradation occurring
with unprecedented delicateness. What is found in such
an instance is this: The individual eachness of posture of
the petals of the opening manifold has a double aspect;
in some particular—a color surface, a direction, a nextness
—it is like its neighbor, and in another aspect—its posture
and its own peculiar location and shadow—it is different.
In its aspect of sameness, the mind finds satisfaction and
rest; but its uniqueness is an aspect that is not matched or

repeated anywhere in the rose and is thus left in a state of potency not actualized; the mind reaches for actualization of relation unfulfilled, but it is at the same time drawn to rest in the samenesses in the whole. While each petal of the multiple centric manifold is related to all the others and seen as a small substructure of the structure, each is seen also as structure of which some elements are sameness interrelated (right correspondent with left, right-left proportionate with top-bottom), others are samenesses with other petals (shape to shape, color gradation to color gradation) and with the rose as a whole (here to there, there to there, there to here). The other elements of the structure of each individual petal are those that are unlike the others, that are unshared by the rest of the whole structure and hence left at the stage of potential or unactualized relationship. When the viewer is looking at the individual petal, but held by its samenesses and its differentness from the rest, the relation with the others and with the whole are momentarily apprehended as elements of the structure of the petal. The visual action shifts or oscillates between seeing a whole structure (of the rose) of which the petal is an element, and, in another view, seeing the petal as a structure of which the others and the whole rose are elements. The petal is an element (substructure) one minute, a structure the next; the rose is a structure one minute, an element the next.

When the petal is seen as a structure, two aspects of it are felt to war against each other; the samenesses with other petals and with the whole rose war against the deviation from sameness, the petal's uniqueness of posture and placement. The mind clings to the uniqueness, loving deviation, and then presently oscillates to the vision of the rose as a structure of which all petals are parts, subsumes all samenesses and all deviations. Perhaps a new appearance becomes clear: all differences are differences and in being so they are the same, and in the case of petals, they are felt as half-differences. In other words, the mind finds a new unity and is pleased. Unity is freshly experienced as the principle of the rose's structure; and then, in the deviant petal, which curls as far away as it can toward the stem, the unity of the rose is threatened. The deviant petal is like other petals in ways other than that of position and posture; even in position and posture it is somewhat like all the others (being attached at its point, following the norm of more and more outward), and the mind, secure in that, travels the proportions of the petal as structure. It reaches toward the direction of deviation, as far as the petal can take it to awayness. But awayness implies the norms from which it leans away, and the mind—which is in a lively, exploratory state of "esthetic awareness"—reaches back to the momentarily relinquished norm of unity; it has shifted its focus to seeing the deviant petal now as an element of the rose's structure; again, unity is freshly experienced as the principle of the rose and confirmed in the seeing of the deviant petal as related to the other deviant, and these in relation to the centric multiplicity.

When the mind adverts to the structure of the rose of which the petal substructures are elements, it is seeing a complex of values as one esthetic whole; when it seeks the vision of the structure of the petal of which the rose is an element, it is enjoying an individual structural value. The petal is affirmed and validated by the rose, and the rose is intensified, complicated, and thus esthetically validated by the deviant. Value emanates at once from the system (the rose), of which the valuable entity (the petal) is representative, and from the unique purity of the entity (the petal's own individual curl toward the stem). The esthetic value is actualized by the relationship between the extremity of the deviation and the rose's structural unity. The rose claims the deviation, and the deviation is valuable because it is not lost to the rose (the petal, though leaning as far as it can, is a part of it).

Once the mind has felt the system (the unity of the rose) reaffirmed, it is exhilarated. Unity is the noticeable thing. The tightness of this unity is increased by illusion resulting from reaction to hazard. The reaction seems like cognitive apprehension, but it is affective impulse at the glimpse of interrelations. A test of the value is the length of time that the mind can still be found to love it, to remember and relive it, or to be interested in it. Another is its power to drive the mind with the excitement of contemplating it. And, paradoxically, the durability and power of the esthetic value both issue from a triumph of fragility or, in other words, the almost-too-hazardous-hazards overcome.

It is not only in the advertence to one petal and then the whole structure that oscillation in the mind's response to the rose is noticed. The mind abstracts the aspect of color value by adverting to color, brightness, and shadow, to a greater and lesser degree of intensity of hue, and so forth. Again, the mind abstracts the aspect of softness of texture, seeing it structurally as sameness and difference of degree. In such instances as these, the aspect abstracted from its embeddedness in the system of the rose's structure as a whole is seen as a structure, as the petal was, but now the elements of the abstracted structure are drawn from all the petals, all parts of the total structure. The deviation from the norm of unity is found now in the differentness of norms implied by the new structure, namely, independent norms of the theory of color or those of texture. The mind finds that the independent system of norms which govern color give new life to its experience of the rose, and the system of structural unity of the rose affirms and occasions a deep intuitional insight into the nature of color. Color value, although based on scientific norms of color, is felt as an effect of the structural value of the rose, and the esthetic value of the rose is felt as a qualification of the theory of color. This is experienced as the attention oscillates between the two systems of norms—the structure of the rose and the science of color.

Sometimes in a lyric, a small noticeable word carries the current from the deviant to the system. For instance, in Shakespeare's line from Sonnet 18: "When in eternal lines to time thou growest," the reader is stopped by the word *to*, because usually one says *for a* time, *during that* time, but not *to* time. The stop occasions a look around, and the idea occurs that *growing to* something means being engrafted. Could it be intentional? It seems so, because the growing will be achieved by a life that is borrowed from union with something "eternal," the poem's lines. The person addressed by the poem will be immortalized, increased with the passing of time by being celebrated by the poem. This is a paradox, because the passing of time is usually attended by decrease and death. But the line suggests grafting and new increasing life. The reader looks for other signs of grafting and suddenly finds an antithesis in the same sonnet's third line: "Rough winds do shake the darling buds of May," where beautiful life is ruthlessly destroyed by separation from the tree. The fallen buds will fade. The reader notices "But thy eternal beauty shall not fade," and then several lines later, "Nor shall Death brag thou wanderest in his shade," or "Every fair from fair sometime declines," and observes, in the whole, the fading of life and beauty, the passing of time, the bustle of rough winds, and the silent growing to time. Noisy and ruthless force destroys beauty, and careful quiet art generates it. The mind is lured by meaning which widens and deepens in all directions. This means that the systems of reference provided by experiences of life and reality open up endlessly.

Meanwhile, in every line the sound is noticeable. The sound of *t* in *eternal*, and in *time*, words so opposite in meaning, magnetizes attention, and sounds begin to grow clear—*fair* . . . *fair* . . . *fade* . . . *shade* . . . *compare* . . . *day* . . . *May* . . . *date* . . . the almost-reaching rhyme of *temperate*, which even in its meaning represents almost-ness, not-quiteness.

There is no end to the freshening lure of assonance and rhyme. The system of qualitative sound hints at the existence of more unexplored; so does the system of quantitative sound structure, and so does the system of an-

tithesis and paradox, all appearing as the mind oscillates
between the part and the whole of the structure.[130] The
strictures of pattern prevent the freedom to explore meanings merely suggested, and pattern recurrences lure the
divided attention. The nature of the sonnet, the nature of
form, of language, and of art are all given affirmation, and
each is a whole system.[131]

In the exhilaration that accompanies the discovery of
systems, values are suffused, and response swiftly advances
to completeness. This experience is common to those who
do and to those who do not go on to evaluate. Response
is not evaluation. Evaluation requires more.

Knowledge of the money system helps one to evaluate
the quarter; knowing the language helps one to evaluate
the word; the philosopher can best evaluate the ultimate
insight; the moralist can assess the value of the action; the
scientist can best recognize the implications of a hypothesis and evaluate the accuracy of proof. Knowledge is required.

But the evaluative judgement is directed to relation
between the unique particular and the system. Moreover,
the evaluator needs only as much knowledge of the system
as is relevant to the unique entity, and his knowledge can
pass without experimental proof, being to a certain extent
estimative and intuitive. It is true that his hypothetical
reaches are less foolproof than those of a learned scientist
who knows the system.

Insofar as evaluative judgments are judgments, they
are particular applications of some knowledge; but they do
not call on full and firm knowledge so much as on cognition supplementing relevant knowledge. Furthermore, although this is true of the evaluative judgment, it must not
be taken as true of criticism. The ideal critic must have
full and accurate scientific knowledge. His work is not only
an initial evaluative judgment as such, although such
judgment is an important phase of it. He examines his
initial evaluatory statement to see whether the reality
evaluated warrants it. Any intelligent and perceptive per-

son makes an evaluatory statement, but a critic must know not only whether value is present, but what it is. He defines and assesses the particular value of the object.

In every instance of value the system identifies it in respect to kind.[132] The differentiation of the degree of value of a particular object can be determined only by seeing clearly (1) the relation between the particular occurrence and the system; (2) the particular in its own context; and (3) the system in its centrality, complexity, and scope. Although the occurrence of value hinges upon the relationship itself between the particular and the system,

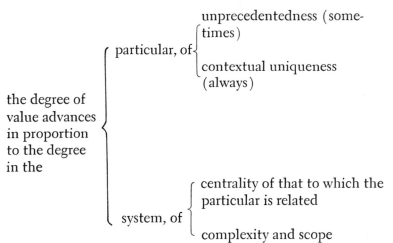

the degree of value advances in proportion to the degree in the

particular, of — unprecedentedness (sometimes)

contextual uniqueness (always)

system, of — centrality of that to which the particular is related

complexity and scope

In the critical evaluating of a thing, it is necessary to keep all of these factors in view; neglect of one or more of them with corresponding stress upon another has damaged criticism at times, rendering it perhaps "too subjective" or "too objective."[133] Although value is possible to an object under certain conditions, independently of our minds, it is not wholly objective, for the conditions are essentially relationships, and relationship is not actualized unless found by the mind. As for affectivity, it accompanies apprehension of value because the relationships that constitute value are hazardous. But feeling is not the criterion of value, not even of esthetic value, as Richards claimed it was.

A value, being relationship between a particular occurrence and a system, cannot be said to be absolute. The particular, which is individuated by its matter and its context and related to the general, is relative on account of its matter and context, contingent in its dependency on the actualizing recognition by the mind for its relationship to a system, and subjective in the sense that the degree of its individuation depends for its value on a mind's perceptiveness to realize it. But some generalities of the system can be absolute (usually they are not, for experiment keeps modifying knowledge of systems). In some systems the relations can be necessary, and systems based on orderly real relationship among objective realities are in that sense objective. Thus, value is never wholly one thing or the other, its nature being characterized by relevant inclusiveness and involvement.

Critics have tended to stress one value of the esthetic complex to the prejudice of the others and in so doing have left a misleading impression. In times of religious and philosophical skepticism, there is a tendency to put undue stress upon philosophical or theological value in the arts; but a vast amount of exquisite artistic form has only negligible philosophical or theological value. Again, the relative stress laid by critics upon the extenuated particular issues in the modern tendency to exclude from notice anything but the quality of an experience in literature,[134] and to magnify experience per se.

Experience and "experiment" have so secure a reputation of importance as to be frequently referred to as "cult." Its popularity has had an effect, of one kind or another, upon practically every thinking and unthinking person. Experience is immemorially "the best teacher," and the reason that the old adage has had so long a life is that the mind finds it true, and life proves it so.[135] Nevertheless, commitments made to experience by pedagogues and psy-

chologists, hence journalists, and hence the public, have
not brought to society the promised reward in the form of
maturity. The paradox of a society of unprecedented experience and of unprecedented immaturity suggests that
experience as such, simple though it seems, is not clearly
understood.

When Blake called his lyrics "Songs of Innocence" and
"Songs of Experience," the dichotomy reflected a concept
of each which has ancient roots in a philosophical over-
simplification. In present ideas about value in art, it turns
up as hardy as ever. The dichotomy alone suggests a dilemma: in one way, "experience" of evil which is survived
seems better than the "innocence" of remaining "inexpe-
rienced," because of itself experience tends to mature the
human being. Nobody wants to remain immature, even if
maturity is costly. In another sense, in actual practice the
end does not justify the means, and to perform an evil act
for experience of evil or for the sake of maturing is per-
verted. In the presence of the dilemma, to compromise by
small concessions to evil, while it is not strictly a deliberate
perversion because it is so often befogged, is nevertheless
eventually discovered to be stunting and not maturing in
its effect on human beings.

Since the time of Blake there have been innumerable
proofs that the cult of experience, by this time increased
and multiplied through union with the romantic cult of
feeling, has rendered the idea of adult innocence idiotic.
Contemporary literature, theater, and film provide fictional
lives of experience through stages of advancing jadedness.
While exceedingly civilized men respond to the values in
contemporary fiction and recognize them, what they recognize is not correspondent with what the characters in
the piece are presuming. That even the author himself is
the most knowing reader of his own novel is not a foregone
conclusion. On the evidence of some works, where attitude
toward experience is clear, an answer to the question of
whether evil might be conceded to, since it provides ex-

perience, seems hinted at; but in others where it is left ambiguous, it is not possible to answer.

The work of Hemingway, for example, is sometimes characterized by a clear attitude, as in *A Farewell to Arms,* and at other times left ambiguous, as in *The Short Happy Life of Francis Macomber.* In the latter the character Wilson thinks that Macomber has reached maturity overnight under powerful pressures he feels following an encounter with a lion and with his wife's rejection. Whether or not Hemingway would consider this likely one cannot be sure, since Wilson is not Hemingway and Macomber is dead a few seconds after his sudden supposed maturation, making proof impossible. But the usual reader accepts Wilson's commentary on the matter without question, because Wilson is the most successful and competent person in the story, and because Macomber has changed from a state of being afraid of a lion and of his wife's disapproval to the state of indifference to his wife and exhilaration at the onrush of a buffalo. A buffalo presents no small peril, and exhilaration at such a moment is a demonstration not to be taken lightly. So Wilson's summary diagnosis that the young man had reached maturity, rendered in a capsule of Wilson's peculiar brand of understatement, fixes the impression (before the dazzled mind has had a chance to evaluate the situation) that Macomber's short moment of adventure was "happy," and at last he had arrived. Experience, perilous and (this especially) *felt* to the hilt, matured him. If Wilson's observation is to be approved as valid, then drug addiction, illicit sex indulgence, rioting, and machine-gunning mature a person.

The definition of experience ventured by Henry James in his preface to *The Princess Casamassima* requires more than that implied by Wilson. James writes, "Experience, as I see it, is our apprehension and our measure of what happens to us as social creatures—any intelligent report of which has to be based on that apprehension."[136] We must apprehend or see what has happened, and we must somehow take measure of it. Taking the drug is not the best teacher; it merely supplies the best teacher with the text to work on; the teacher is the apprehension and the measurement of the act. Moreover, it does not always have to be apprehension and measurement of one's own act to issue in maturity; it has only to be one's own apprehension and one's own measurement. Precisely because this is true literature can have some of the values that it sometimes has, and, more broadly considered, any values at all. In other words, it is not what happens to us or what we ostensibly do that constitutes maturing experience, but rather those happenings properly interpreted, related to systems.

Since relationship is actualized by the mind, it is by man that actual value is preserved. Moreover, because the power of a work of art is experienced as the source of excitement, value being necessarily a relationship that is hazardous, it is for men that the power of value is rendered actual. Value, therefore, although dependent for its occasion on objective systems and event or entities, is nevertheless initiated, realized, and brought to full flower, in immanent human activity. This would seem at first glance to be contradicted by instances of value-in-exchange, such as that of money. But even value-in-exchange is exchange of values.[137]

Response to art can prove exacting, for the coexistence of conflicting values in the structure of a work of art produces "tension" by luring the receiver to two or more separate values, each constituting a hazard for the others, and the lure of them all being the crucial hazard sustained by the primary value of the object. The sovereignty of each value in its own proper sphere is absolute.

Therefore, a thing of great scientific value or great artistic value cannot be said not to have those values because the fact or the work is immoral. The evaluator would have to say it has great scientific value, it has great artistic value, but it is immoral. To say each of these three things with scientific authority takes a good deal of knowledge (of systems) and judgmental acumen (estimates of the particular and intelligence of its relevance to the systems).

However, the realization of value is not to be despaired of until vast accumulation of specialized knowledge can be acquired, since in the relating of the particular entity to the system, only one aspect of relatedness is evoked; in the contemplating of this, one finds other facets appearing, as the systemic implications open up, and if they continue to do so, the value is genuine and enduring.

Such responding to value is possible for any normal and especially any gifted human being. The critic, however, must have thorough knowledge of the system on which a value depends as well as the gifted person's perceptiveness to go the whole way with the particular and to apprehend the relationship between the two.

So far we have seen that in valuable occurrence, a particular entity or event is related to the centrality of a system of which it is representative. However, it appears too that the particular, although momentarily viewed in isolation, really belongs to a system of its own. When a value is experienced, a whole sequence of factors is present, although not consciously adverted to. The money is related to the bread; next, the money is seen to have buying power because it has a monetary system behind it. The bread appears to be an isolated particular because it is viewed only in its relation to the coin. But in reality it is desirable as part of a system of the daily routine of eating, and this to the physical system of the body nourished by the bread, and this in turn to the possibilities attendant upon prolongation of life in the body, and so on.

This raises the question of whether valuable occurrence is a locus where system meets system. It would seem that it is; what this comes to, since value is relationship found by the mind, is that it is an instance of relatedness where the mind experiences the lures of both systems, oscillates in its action, exploring the implications (systemic relations) in both directions, while staying with the particular which is invested with value, since it is the occasion of contact. Frequently, especially in the case of esthetic value, one of the systems is intuited rather than explicable at the moment of value.

Even without knowledge of two fields of study, if a person has a good command of one, so that knowing the particulars of its system he can also see relationships among them and relationships between all this and a crucial fact of another field of study, value is likely to attend the insight into that connection. Schrecker, seeing analogous structures (isomorphs) in the different areas of civilization, demonstrates the affirmation of each area by every other, views their interaction, and sees civilization itself as a dynamic structure. Moreover, he is enabled thereby to make observations about nature, by contrast. So broad a scope is hazardous, and exhilarating, too, not a safe condition for scientific accuracy. But when history confirms the principles and is illuminated by them in turn, the authenticity is clear. The advantage of comparative or interdisciplinary studies is that they seed hypotheses, and inquiry is thus given tentative direction.[138]

This broad exhilarating scope, a modern way of entertaining the sublime, is the playground of youthful scientists; meanwhile, the arts romantically cling to the dark where they can be infinitely and imaginatively extended. Of the two the scientists prosper more because at least they work in the light and with structure and can move from m to n and thus from m^2 to n^2, whereas the modern artist who repudiates form must loudly affirm the existence of cosmic mystery, or absurdity, his entire proof resting upon the enormity of the lengths to which he is willing to go.

But by trying to render art absolute and all-encompassing, annihilating boundaries and system, the romantic artist destroys value. It is the organization of the units in series that creates perspective, for instance. The viewer, seeing the potencies in perspective, takes them further, and what is artfully excluded by the artistic process is important, because negatively that, too, directs responsive action to virtually infinite horizons.

Even should it be conceded to the romanticist that art should be the cosmic open sesame, the cosmos itself is implied to be system. All reality is more or less structured. This appears even in the antithesis between the immensity of the cosmos and the mind of man. The antithesis can in fact be patly demonstrated by juxtaposing Newton's law of universal gravitation (cosmic reality) and that of affective hazard (the mind):

Every body in the universe attracts every other body with a force that is *inversely* proportional to the square of the distance between them.	Everything in the universe is related to every other thing with excitement that is *directly* proportional to the square of distance (obstacle, hazard) between them.

This makes no claim to mystery, since it is natural for the human being to become habituated to the ways of things surrounding him, thus to find rarefaction of reference hazardous and the delayed actualization of it joyous. But it seems true that each of these laws affirms the other. If they do, it is a case of inverted analogy between a fact of physics and a fact of psychology, and suggests the possibility of more.

So large a supposition can be entertained if there is order or structure in the universe; the artist can create form and thus incarnate value. Because it seems to be a law of both life and art that extremity of hazard threatening form, and paradoxically serving to organize it so that unity is found with always fresh astonishment to have been inevitable, endows the object with perennial increase of value. However, if there is no order in the universe, one can frame an amorphous splash on a canvas, blindly affirming the "universe" of Democritus, and then anticipating a revelation from it with impunity. For if there is no system, there is at least no harm in waiting with futile hope for the flesh to become word.

Notes

1. "Essay on Homer's Battles," *The Iliad of Homer Translated by Mr. Pope* (London: printed by W. Bowyer for Bernard Lintot between the Temple-Gates, 1715), 2, 324.
2. In *The Art of the Novel,* ed. Richard P. Blackmur (New York: Charles Scribner's Sons, 1953), p. 164. References to James's prefaces to his novels are from this edition, unless otherwise noted.
3. *The Liberal Imagination* (New York: Viking Press, 1950), p. 187.
4. "The Cutting of an Agate." *Essays* (New York: Macmillan, 1924), p. 33. See also, Donald A. Stauffer, *The Golden Nightingale* (New York: Macmillan, 1949), pp. 142–43.
5. Pope, "Homer's Battles," 324.
6. Alexander Pope, "Postscript," *The Odyssey of Homer Translated from the Greek* (London: printed for Bernard Lintot, 1726), 5, 304.
7. Alexander Pope, "Preface to the Iliad," *The Prose Works of Alexander Pope,* ed. Norman Ault (Oxford: The Shakespeare Head Press, 1936): 1, 240.
8. *On the Sublime,* ed., trans. W. Rhys Roberts, 2nd ed. (Cambridge: at the University Press, 1907), 9. 5.
9. Ibid., 36. 1.
10. Joseph Addison, ed., *The Spectator* (Cincinnati: Applegate and Company, 1862), #414, June 25, 1712.
11. *The Rhetoric of Aristotle,* trans. Lane Cooper (New York: Appleton-Century-Crofts, 1932), 1404b5.
12. Aristotle, *De Anima, in the Version of William of Moerbeke and The Commentary of St. Thomas Aquinas* trans. Kenelm Foster and Silvester Humphries (London: Routledge and Kegan Paul, 1951), 431b5. Hereinafter cited as *De Anima—Commentary.*
13. *On the Sublime,* 23. 2.
14. *Essays,* 339.
15. note to 10. 584.
16. *Odyssey,* note to 12. 222.

17. Alexander Pope, Letter to Wycherly, Dec. 26, 1704, *The Works of Alexander Pope*, ed. Elwin and Courthope (London: John Murray, 1871), 6, 16.

18. Wing-tsit-Chan, "Expression," *Encyclopedia of the Arts*, ed. Dagobert Runes and Harry Schrickel (New York: Philosophical Library, 1946), p. 339.

19. *On the Art of Poetry*, ed., trans. Ingram Bywater (Oxford: Clarendon Press, 1909), 1448b9–10.

20. Ibid., 1448b13ff.; see also *Rhetoric*, 1371b4–10.

21. In saying interest is "not entirely" traceable to the differentness of the natures of the two things that are related, I mean to suggest that it is traceable also to the "psychical distance" noticed by Edward Bullough, in his " 'Psychical Distance' as a Factor in Art and an Aesthetic Principle," a 1912 essay reprinted in *Aesthetics: Lectures and Essays by Edward Bullough*, ed. Elizabeth M. Wilkinson (Stanford, Calif.: Stanford University Press, 1957), especially pp. 94, 96, 114.

22. *Rhetoric*, 1417a19.

23. D. W. Robertson, Jr., pointed out in "The Doctrine of Charity in Medieval Literary Gardens," *Speculum* 26 (Jan. 1951), 24, that Saint Augustine, Hugh of Saint Victor, Petrarch, and Boccaccio were aware of the pleasurableness of meaning that comes to the mind, so managed as to be apprehended only with difficulty.

24. *Rhetoric*, 1370a31–b5. The lines from the Odyssey are 15, 398–401. Stauffer, p. 81, emphasizes the moment of cognition as that of pleasure in his insistence that a poem, once it is become "act . . . should give us . . . the reflected pleasure, that comes from participating in a successful accomplishment." The poem "become act" is cognitive meaning so subtly managed as to achieve a very nearly miraculous organization of hazards. A simpler and clear contemporary pronouncement of this particular aspect of the principle is that of Walter Ong, "Metaphor and the Twinned Vision," *Sewanee Review* 63 (Spring 1955), 198, 199, who notices a certain type of far-fetched metaphor that is most "effective," provided "that somehow the distance between the widely divergent meanings can be effectively bridged." In other words given the intrinsic hazard of wide divergence, the metaphor becomes exciting "provided that somehow" cognition occurs.

25. *Works*, 6, 213–14.

26. René Wellek and Austin Warren, *The Theory of Literature* (New York: Harcourt, Brace, 1949), p. 251.

27. Some years ago I heard Ants Oras, in a context pertaining to sound in poetry, use the apt term "rarity value," at the English Institute, 1955, at Columbia University, New York.

28. "Form," *Dictionary of World Literature*, ed. Joseph T. Shipley (New York: The Philosophical Library, 1943), p. 250.

29. "Structure, Sound and Meaning," *Sound and Poetry*, ed. Northrop Frye (New York: Columbia University Press, 1957), p. 89.

30. LaDrière, "Literary Form and Form in the Other Arts," *Stil-und*

Formprobleme in der Literatur, ed. Paul Böckmann (Heidelberg, 1959), p. 32.

31. Cf. René Wellek, "Concepts of Form and Structure in Twentieth Century Criticism, *Neophilologus*, 42 (1958), 2–11.

32. Charles Lalo, "The Aesthetic Analysis of a Work of Art," *JAAC*, 7 (Summer 1949), 277, points out in an examination of a very small unit of a poem "Five main elemental (we do not say: atomic) structures make up the counterpoint at least of five voices that may be heard harmoniously singing in this couplet: The five sub-structures in this superstructure are: the explicit verbal meanings, subconscious suggestions, logical, grammatical linkings, and finally rhythms and timbers." In musical structures which become actualized in exclusively temporal sequence, expectancies are evoked "not only within phrases and smaller parts . . . but also between them" and "sub-systems must be analyzed within the larger system," according to Leonard B. Meyer, "Meaning in Music and Information Theory," *JAAC*, 15 (Summer 1957), 421, 422.

33. LaDrière, "Structure, Sound and Meaning," p. 87; See also, LaDrière's "Literary Form," pp. 33–35.

34. *De Anima—Commentary*, 2. 1. 224.

35. Ibid., 2. 1. 218.

36. "Significant Form," *Proceedings of the IV International Congress on Aesthetics*, p. 739.

37. When the artist is able to produce a form that has that power, the esthetic interest that results is "interest as form for direct contemplation." The only principle of esthetic structure is that of "internal consistency," noticed in the "play of relations," in patterns of "samenesses and differences, of likeness and unlikeness." Structure is necessarily "constituted by relations" and a structure whose "whole principle of organization is aesthetic is a structure simply of relations, a structure in terms of relations simply as such." LaDrière, "Structure, Sound and Meaning," pp. 99, 100, "Literary Form," p. 32, respectively.

38. "Concepts of Form," p. 5

39. LaDrière, "Form," p. 250.

40. LaDrière, "Literary Form," p. 29: There are "always two things to be considered in dealing with form in the arts . . . the material upon which the artist works" or "the elements . . . organized . . . into a given form, and . . . the form or structure itself into which these elements are organized. . . . The primary questions . . . are . . . 'What are the elements which are here organized together,' and, second, 'By what principle of association or order are they so organized, and into what structure?' "

41. LaDrière, "Comparative Method in the Study of Prosody," *Comparative Literature, Proceedings of the ICLA Congress*, ed. W. P. Friederich (Chapel Hill: University of North Carolina Press, 1949), p. 10.

42. Ferdinand de Saussure, *Cours de linguistique générale* (Paris, 1922), p. 166.

43. LaDrière, "Literary Form," p. 30.

44. LaDrière, "Comparative Method," p. 10.
45. Harold Osborne, *Aesthetics and Criticism* (New York: The Philosophical Library, 1955), p. 277.
46. Meyer, p. 418, says an event is hypothetical when the consequents are still in the condition of being expected; as soon as the consequent is apprehended by the mind, the relationship is evident. Determinate meanings arise "when all the implications of the stimulus . . . are realized and their interrelationships comprehended."
47. De Saussure, p. 103. See also pp. 170–71.
48. The convenience of the terminology representing the just-before, the during, and the just-after is its aptness to anything progressive. Even in the submolecular relationship (that of the signifying to the signified) central to semiosis, the signification registering in the reader's mind goes through the three phases palpably, sometimes producing excitement, depending upon the condition of the occurrence. Hamlet, in his famous soliloquy beginning "To be or not to be," says that it is the uncertainty of what lies beyond the grave that "puzzles the will." This interests the attentive mind: the hypothetical signification at the moment *puzzles* registers, is expectation of the word *mind*. The mind properly experiences a dilemma in being puzzled. But *the will* occurs instead of *the mind*, the expresed thing deviating from the hypothetical signification: immediately, in this compression of puzzles-the-mind-which-dictates-to-the-will-with-the-result-that-the-will-cannot-choose to *puzzles the will*, the reader's mind is reined in and experiences awareness. This prepares it to see the determinate meaning, namely, the retrospective grasp of the implication that for Hamlet mind and will are paralyzed by the depth of his uncertainty; and as this is apprehended to fit the totality of the play, widening determinate meaning is achieved.
49. De Saussure gives associative relationship as the alternative to a relationship that is syntagmatic. Unlike syntagmatic agreement, which is linear, associative agreement tends to lure the notice away from the linear track. It differs from the syntagmatic by being indeterminate in order, although the order peculiar to it can be traceable. It is indefinite also in number. A preposition has syntagmatic relationship with its object (notwithstanding opposition) and associative agreement with other words of the same root (understanding) or suffix (considering) or signification (in spite of), or acoustic images in common, either qualitative (top this landing) or quantitative (on that premise) or both (not this landing). Associative relationship can therefore beckon from many directions and militate against syntagmatic direction of attention; and this can go on in a simple sentence. The simplest sentence is already far removed from simplicity. Consequently, when the poet uses language as the matter upon which he imposes form, especially form as systematized relationship of sameness and difference, relationship is inexhaustible. Since the mind, the instrument which discovers and thus actualizes relationship, can attend to only one thing at a time and yet can out of the corner of its eye, so to speak, perceive the front ranks

of hosts of others, it appears that, as Eva Schaper and René Wellek have both said, the art form becomes a system of "potencies."

50. LaDrière, "Literary Form," pp. 29–32.

51. Aquinas, *De Anima*—Commentary, 2. 7. 315.

52. *Vision and Design* (London: Chatto and Windus, 1929), p. 52.

53. Aquinas, *Summa Theologica*, trans. Fathers of the English Dominican Province (New York: Benziger Brothers, 1947), 1. 28. 4.

54. Ibid., 1. 42. 1. ad 2.

55. Ibid., 28. 2. obj. 3.

56. The poet's creating of a contingent subjective relationship between two things which are not related or relatable in reality is legitimate; but the proper response to it is to be alert to the implications of that relating. They are not likely to be the same as those of metaphors linking relatable things, because the reader is living in a world whose reality has been impressing itself upon him through his five senses for years. The intelligibility of metaphors of subjective contingent relationship is based upon the fact that emotional connections are dimly intelligible to sharers of human nature. But the reading of modern poetry which makes use of subjective and contingent relationship in metaphor is not the same kind of experience as that of the reading of Sonnet 18 by Shakespeare.

57. Aquinas, *Summa Theologica*, 1. 28. 1.

58. Ibid., 1. 47. 3. The non-regressiveness of the entropy of the physical universe referred to by the second law of thermodynamics is in itself a kind of predictability (order).

59. *The Poetry of Ezra Pound* (Norfolk, Conn.: New Directions, n.d.), p. 99.

60. Erich Heller, "Parody, Tragic and Comic: Mann's *Doctor Faustus* and *Felix Krull*," *Sewanee Review*, 56 (Summer 1958), 531–32.

61. Meaning as such is simply a relationship of reference, different from reality in this respect, that its related terms and their relatableness do not have to (although they may) exist in reality outside the mind. When they do exist in reality, this does not directly affect the poem as a poem. Sound and meaning are shaped into a structure, and that is what the critic must be able to give an account of.

62. Aquinas, *Summa Theologica*, 1. 30. 1.

63. Meyer, p. 415.

64. When Susanne Langer, for whom the semblance of form "seems to be charged with reality," calls the meaning the "vital import," she is talking about the same thing. The semblance in the mind is charged with what seems to be reality when it is intensely particularized and coherent, because these two conditions so engage the mind that it relinquishes its hold on critical inquiry. And meaning "of vital import" is affectively charged, a form to which feeling is at least not foreign. That "context" and "form" can be considered the same is not unlikely (*Feeling and Form* [New York: Charles Scribner's Sons, 1953], 52).

65. Aquinas, *Summa Theologica*, 1. 40. 2.

66. Ibid., 1. 30. 1.

67. Ibid., 1. 40. 2: In instances of relationship, "the correlative" is "not prior but simultaneous in the order of nature."

68. "Meaning in Music," p. 417.

69. Samuel Coleridge, *Coleridge's Shakesperean Criticism*, ed. Thomas Middleton Raysor (London: Constable and Company, 1930), 1, 223–24.

70. Stauffer, 110.

71. *The Sacred Wood*, 6th ed. (London: Methuen, 1946), pp. 168–69.

72. Henry James, "Preface to *The Ambassadors*," p. 326.

73. Robert O. Preyer, "Julius Hare and Coleridgean Criticism," *JAAC*, 15 (Summer 1957), 450.

74. James, "Preface to *The Ambassadors*," pp. 317–18.

75. Gerard Manley Hopkins, "Poetic Diction," *A Hopkins Reader*, ed. John Pick (New York: Oxford University Press, 1953), p. 80.

76. Victor Erlich, *Russian Formalism* ('S-Gravenhage: Mouton, 1955), p. 200.

77. Ibid., p. 172.

78. Kenner, p. 93.

79. Meyer H. Abrams, *The Mirror and the Lamp* (New York: Oxford University Press, 1953), p. 174.

80. Meyer, pp. 420–21.

81. Curt Sachs, *The Rise of Music in the Ancient World* (New York: W. W. Norton, 1943), p. 37.

82. *Poetry of Ezra Pound*, p. 103.

83. Aristotle, *Politics*, *The Basic Works of Aristotle*, ed. Richard McKeon, 1254a29–33. This inequality is everywhere, and it is indispensable to value. The best agent is the one who produces an "effect which is best in its entirety," not making "every part of the whole the best absolutely, but in proportion to the whole; in the case of an animal, for instance, its goodness would be taken away if every part of it had the dignity of an eye." (Aquinas, *Summa Theologica*, 1. 47. 2. *Reply to Obj.* 1). In fact, "inequality comes from the perfection of the whole. This appears also in works done by art." (Ibid., *Reply to Obj.* 3). Rudolph Arnheim sees "hierarchy" to be at least a "minimum demand on a work of art" in "Accident and the Necessity of Art," *JAAC*, 16 (Fall 1957), p. 27, and the consciousness of its necessity is present in those critics of Impressionist paintings referred to by Mercier, who complain that the "pictures, though crowded with faithful notations of reality, offer no one point in the composition where the eye can rest and around which the remainder of the picture can be focused." See Vivian Mercier, "The Limitations of Flaubert," *Kenyon Review*, 19 (Summer 1957), p. 407.

84. *Painting*—John Dryden, "A Parallel of Poetry and Painting," *Essays of John Dryden*, ed. W. P. Ker (Oxford: Clarendon Press, 1900): 2, 151. See also, Samuel Johnson, "Milton," *Works*, 9, 177; Pope, note to *Iliad* 5. 1ff.; note to *Odyssey*, 8, 510, *Poetry*—Samuel Johnson, *Rambler* #150, *Works*, 6, 60; *Novel*—Henry James, "Preface to *The Spoils of Poynton*," p. 136; cf. Mercier; *Architecture*—Pope, "Epistle IV," *Works*, 3, 180, ll. 109–10:

"Lo what huge heaps of littleness around!
The whole, a laboured quarry above ground."

85. James, "Preface to *Roderick Hudson*," p. 14.
86. Paul Schrecker, *Work and History* (Princeton: Princeton University Press, 1948), p. 132; cf. LaDrière, "Structure, Sound and Meaning," pp. 92, 97, 98; also, "Literary Form," pp. 31–37.
87. Paul Klee as quoted by Étienne Gilson, *Painting and Reality* (New York: Pantheon Books, 1957), p. 123, n. 16.
88. Dryden, p. 145.
89. Joseph Frank, "Spatial Form in the Modern Novel," in *Critiques and Essays in Modern Fiction, 1920–1951*, ed. J. W. Aldridge (New York: The Ronald Press, 1952), pp. 43–66; cf. Wellek and Warren, "Literature and Ideas," in *The Theory of Literature*, pp. 107–23.
90. "Montage," in *Essays in Modern Fiction*, p. 143.
91. "John Dos Passos and the Whole Truth," in *Essays in Modern Fiction*, p. 183.
92. Osborne, *Aesthetics and Criticism*, p. 237.
93. Samuel Taylor Coleridge, "Shakespeare, A Poet Generally," *Coleridge's Lectures on Shakespeare and Other Poets and Dramatists*, ed. Ernest Rhys (New York: E. P. Dutton, 1907), p. 46.
94. Hilaire Hiler, "The Origin and Development of Structural Design," *JAAC*, 15 (Sept. 1956), 106–109. The contrast of environment emphasizes its character. The smooth white structure characterized by the stability of the Greek temple was set among green shrubbery, on an irregular mountain, under passing clouds, thus stressing its fixity; the organic structure of much of the new architecture is set among vertical and horizontal lines of buildings which accentuate its curved wavelike manner.
95. Sister Mary Francis Slattery, "Functional Value and Artistic Value," *Proceedings of the IV International Congress on Aesthetics*, ed. P.A. Michelis (Athens, Greece, 1960), p. 208. In the machine's unity, where interconnections are perceived to be unchanging and to be relied upon, there is no affective impact to aid illusory increase of unity. On the other hand, the reason why Cubism has an interest of its own, although apparently imitating fixity, is that unlike the machine, it exploits hazards in illusions of perspective, and in color quality.
96. "Epistle 4" *Works*, 3, 180, ll. 113–18. When musical norms become ends in themselves, there is a "tedium of maximum certainty" (Meyer, p. 419) and structure "is neutral with regard to meaning" (Ibid., p. 415). The "undesirable preponderance of repetitive elements" is "monotony" (Karl Aschenbrenner, "Aesthetic Theory—Conflict and Conciliation," *JAAC*, 18 [Sept. 1959], 96).
97. *Commentary on De Anima*, 2. 11. 266.
98. Gilbert K. Chesterton, *The Autobiography of G. K. Chesterton* (New York: Sheed and Ward, 1936), pp. 25–26.
99. Stephen C. Pepper and Karl H. Potter, "The Criterion of Relevancy in Aesthetics: A Discussion," *JAAC*, 16 (Dec. 1957), 214. The "directly stimulated sensory" is actual.
100. Meyer, p. 415, n. 8.

101. It has been seen that in both arts cognition, indispensable though it is, must be proportionately only just enough. Potency or expectancy must be high; and, in both arts, affectivity is evoked by the hazards of relatively prolonged potencies. Such a situation prevails in the delay of a normal or probable consequent occurrence. Sometimes the antecedent, the already expressed, may be ambiguous: several equally probable consequents may be envisaged. If such be the case, potency is doubled, though not temporally. The potencies are simultaneous, and the delay cannot be prolonged. In this instance, the status of actuality (a beat of rhythm, an outcome of a suspenseful situation) is hazardous. If there is no delay and no ambiguity, but rather frustration is experienced in the occurrence of the positively unexpected, the potency expected is shattered by the negation on the part of the actual, and the usurping actuality is attended by other potencies of its own. In all three cases the receiver's response changes from cognitive security to intuition and anxiety, which is still suffused with affectivity lingering from the antecedent occurrence of the actual. Cf. Meyer, p. 415.

102. In response to antecedent-consequent relationship, the expecting mind "becomes aware of the possibility of alternative modes of continuation. It weighs . . . the probabilities of the situation in the light of past events, the present context, and the possible influence of the delay on the future course of events. For . . . one mode . . . still only probable is not certain," and expectation becomes active, estimating the probabilities of an uncertain situation. The concrete actualization reached, the response shifts from expectancy to affective impulse, and, as Meyer says, at such a point "a new stage of meaning is reached" (pp. 415, 417).

103. Feeling and Form, p. 49.

104. Cf. Slattery, "Functional Value and Aesthetic Value," p. 208: the values are the structure; the structure is constituted by the values.

105. "Significant Form," p. 741.

106. "Meaning in Music," p. 416.

107. Feeling and Form, pp. 48–49.

108. Van Meter Ames, "What Is Form?" p. 86, says: "As the solution of a problem sums up earlier stages, so artistic treatment of the solution symbolizes both the difficulty and the victory and perpetuates their intimacy." The words victory and solution here suggest unity, the actualization of relation; difficulty, on the other hand, is hazard. Again, affectivity is connoted by Ames' use of the words victory and perpetuates . . . intimacy. The linking of similarity and difference is noticed repeatedly by authors, and in the neighborhood of the remark about it, there is usually a hint of a result which is in some way affective.

109. Eliseo Vivas, "The Substance of Women in Love," Sewanee Review, 66 (Autumn 1958), 597–98.

110. Osborne says that this stimulation of the faculties of the mind provided by the work of art "is the highest of all human values" (Harold Osborne, Theory of Beauty [London: Routledge and Kegan Paul, 1952] p. 164). The "heightening of consciousness" or "enhancement

of mental vitality . . . is why the experience of beauty is valued. It is valued because it makes us more vividly alive than we otherwise know how to be" (Osborne, *Aesthetics and Criticism*, pp. 228, 229). This tends to emphasize the receiver's response in the presence of value, and, in my opinion, it seems to lean toward instrumentalizing value. The value, though, regardless of how the sensitive poet or the wide-awake receiver may be enhanced by responding to it, is ascribed to the object.

111. LaDrière, "Literary Form," p. 30.

112. Schrecker, p. 59.

113. *The English Novel, Form and Function* (New York: Rinehart, 1953), pp. 80, 223.

114. Geoffrey Tillotson, "Pope and the Common Reader," *Sewanee Review*, 66 (Winter 1958), 59.

115. Robert Wooster Stallman, "Stephen Crane: A Revaluation," *Essays in Modern Fiction*, pp. 258–59.

116. Meyer, p. 423. John Dewey had been distressed to find that literature on the subject ranged from the idea that values are emotional epithets and mere ejaculations to the equally unacceptable idea that "a priori necessary, standardized, rational values are the principles upon which art, science, and morals depend for their validity." Cf. John Dewey, *Theory of Valuation*, Foundations of the Unity of Science, 2 (4) (Chicago: University of Chicago, 1958, 9th Impression), p. 1.

117. Cf. John Laird, *The Idea of Value* (Cambridge: Cambridge University Press, 1929), p. 36: "Relations, not the pure substance of a separable essence, may be the breath of it."

118. Cf. De Saussure, pp. 158–62.

119. James Craig LaDrière, "Scientific Method in Criticism," *Dictionary of World Literature*, p. 509.

120. LaDrière, "Structure, Sound and Meaning," p. 90.

121. Aschenbrenner, p. 98.

122. William Butler Yeats, "Introduction" to *The Oxford Book of Modern Verse 1892–1935* (New York: Oxford University Press, 1936), p. xxv.

123. *English Novel*, p. 197.

124. Edmund Wilson, *Axel's Castle* (New York: Charles Scribner's Sons, 1931), pp. 62–63.

125. *Partial Portraits* (London: Macmillan and Company, 1905), p. 50.

126. Jacques Maritain, "A Maritain Anthology on Art and Poetry," *Thought*, 26 (Autumn 1951), 333.

127. It does not detract from natural objects, nor from art objects, to find the same esthetic values in both. That one is a fact; besides it is reassuring.

128. Aquinas, *Summa Theologica*, 2. 1. 82. 4.

129. A work of art or a beautiful object can be relatively small, quiet, and unobtrusive. It requires of the receiver an initial undivided attention. However, when this has been given, the presence of value in the work may become clear. Formerly unnoticed things flood the mind. It seems true to say that readers want "great" literature, and "great"

art is worth crossing oceans for. Aristotle, when discussing magnificence, digresses for a moment to remark that "as a piece of property
that thing is most valuable which is worth most, gold for instance;
but as a work that which is great and beautiful, because the contemplation of such an object is admirable, and so is that which is
magnificent. So the excellence of a work is magnificence on a large
scale" (*Nicomachean Ethics*, 1122b15–19). Even though he is not
speaking of the greatness of a painting, a poem, or a musical composition here, what he says could be said of a great work of art.
Thomas Aquinas says of greatness: "Quantity is twofold: There is
a quantity of bulk or dimensive quantity which is found only in
corporeal things . . . . There is also a quantity of *virtue* which is
measured according to the perfection of some nature or form." He
quotes Saint Augustine's *De Trinitate*, 6.18, where he says that "in
things which are great, but not in bulk, to be greater is to be
better." In this sense it can be said that an exquisite sonnet is
"greater" literature than a flawed epic, tragedy, or novel. A mountain
of rusting discarded automobiles has "less great" beauty than a rose,
although the former is quantitatively much greater.

130. LaDrière observes about a situation in which grammar, logic, or
rhetoric are brought into relation in esthetically dominated structure:
"Since none of them is ever pure . . . and in each of their structures
there are aspects and relations they have not absorbed, and these of
course offer their own intrinsic possibilities for construction, the im-
partial appetite of the aesthetic interest will attempt to realize these
possibilities" ("Structure, Sound and Meaning," p. 91).

131. A curious fact about the ordinary world appears in its meeting with
the work of art. The ordinary world is made up of things each with
its own qualified thisness, its own unduplicated cluster of aspects, and
when the particularity of each thing is deeply explored, while at the
same time its aspects are experienced in relation to aspects of all the
other things, the ordinary world begins to take on an aspect of the
extraordinary, because value is discovered everywhere in it.

132. Richards said we can differentiate values by three criteria: novelty,
complexity of connections of experiences, and range of our connections of experiences (G. A. Rudolph, "The Aesthetic Field of I. A.
Richards," *JAAC*, 14 [March 1956], 356). The last two refer to some
system that is necessary if value is present. The connection of experiences means the mental relating of them, and this is generalization that produces systematic knowledge. In this second criterion,
therefore, he is observing that system is relevant, and in the third he
advocates that it have scope. As for the novelty, even there it would
appear that Richards was seeing that same sort of constitution of
value as is discussed above, for novelty as particularity, unprecedentedness, "existential" specification, seems attributable to the particular
occurrence of value.

However, the three elements Richards mentions can be said only
with certain qualifications to differentiate values. The presence of all
three, properly situated, is assurance of the presence of value, and

possibly that is all that Richards meant. But for differentiating the kinds of value, only the second need be mentioned. The coin has exchange value only, being related to a money system, the word, linguistic value, being related to a language system. The system identifies the value.

133. One might be inclined to conclude from what has been said of value that by analogy with the kinds mentioned the esthetic value of an object should be constituted by relation between the particular art object and the system of esthetics. But such is not the case. Although the conformity of the style of the object to the general preconceived norms gives some loose and negative assurance of its value, this is not the relationship upon which its distinguishing value principally depends. As we have seen, the primary value of art, the esthetic value, is constituted by the relation between the part of the object and the whole structural system that constitutes the object. It has already been hinted, and Laird confirms it, that "value is . . . not . . . borrowed ready made" (p. 36). Such borrowing was the error of the less astute among the neoclassicists and in more modern times in biases against the representational, perspective, etc.

Another modern misplacement of esthetic value has been the expressionists' attributing of it to the "emotional experience . . . effectively transferred from the mind of the artist to other men" (Osborne, *Aesthetics and Criticism*, pp. 169–70). The "pleasantness and unpleasantness" that are "qualities of experience" (p. 213) are in the receiver; whatever value they have is psychological, not esthetic. This misunderstanding appears more clearly in Rudolph's interpretation of Richards' doctrine: "We can describe synaesthesis as the highest form of value because the perceiver has his feeling-states most thoroughly organized not only within himself but with his environment. The individual is no longer an individual but an integrated segment of his surroundings" (p. 356). Even if this were true, such value would be functional and pragmatic. It seems questionable to value works of art principally for their conformity to a priori norms.

134. Cf. Vivas, pp. 588–632, where appreciation of the "quality of experience" in Lawrence's novel is shown.

135. Dewey's plea for a return to a study of value is implicit in his observation that the "object which *should* be desired (valued) . . . presents itself because past experience has shown that hasty action upon uncriticized desire leads to defeat and possibly to catastrophe." This is wisdom. Actually, it is possible to evaluate even before the completed issue of hasty action, because our minds can intuit norms of the nature of a situation, or because other minds have already systematized norms on the basis of reason and experience. Criteria of evaluation are attainable. Every particular value implies a system on which it depends for its existence, and Dewey in this quotation is using experience as the system. But by saying it "has shown" something (that is, proposing what looks at least like a universal), he implies that the mind abstracts a general norm from particular ex-

periences. Although one might consider the norm he abstracts a bit pragmatic for a permanent ultimate foundation of the moral system, Dewey's insistence on basing consideration of value on recognition of what is shown universally is admirable.

136. James, "Preface to *The Princess Casamassima*," pp. 64–65.

137. Laird, p. 10: "The ratio of exchange presupposes values and cannot of itself constitute them."

138. Outside the boundaries of art, in science, for example, valuable occurrence attends analogy or perhaps an insight illustrative of a principle common to both of two systems. Always system is important to value. David Bidney, "The Concept of Value in Modern Anthropology," in *Anthropology Today*, ed. A. L. Kroeber (Chicago: University of Chicago Press, 1953), pp. 682–99, proposes as alternative methods of anthropology (1) studies based on the idea that each culture must be viewed as an integrated whole; no cultural traits or institutions to be understood apart from a given cultural context; or (2) comparative studies of cultures and their values, to demonstrate universal principles of cultural dynamics and concrete rational norms capable of universal realization. Bidney advocates comparative studies which would demonstrate universal principles. Where universal principles are attained, system is present, and value can be found. Northrop independently had the same idea in the field of jurisprudence, De Saussure in linguistics, LaDrière in prosody. See F. S. C. Northrop, "Cultural Values," in *Anthropology Today*, pp. 668–80.

Index

Sister Mary Francis Slattery, a member of Sisters of Charity, Mount Saint Vincent-on-Hudson in New York, has taught English at the College of Mount Saint Vincent, Catholic University of America, and George Washington University. She now is adjunct assistant professor at George Washington. She is a former editor of the *New Catholic Encyclopedia*. Sister Mary Francis Slattery is a graduate of the College of Mount Saint Vincent (B.A., 1931) and holds the M.A. (1942) and Ph.D. (1951) degrees from Catholic University.

The manuscript was edited by Linda Grant. The book was designed by Joanne Kinney. The type face for the text is linotype Electra designed by W. A. Dwiggins in 1935; and the display face is Garamond designed by Claude Garamond in the 16th century.

The text is printed on Glatfelter's P and S Wove paper and the book is bound in Columbia Mills' Riverside Chambray cloth over binders boards. Manufactured in the United States of America.